D1132565

# Great Ideas for Potters

*Ceramics*
MONTHLY

# Great Ideas for Potters

### Selected from over 30 years of readers' suggestions

Edited by
**Barbara Tipton**

© Copyright 1983

Professional Publications, Inc.
1609 Northwest Boulevard, Columbus, Ohio 43212

*Publishers of* CERAMICS MONTHLY

**First Printing May 1983**
**Second Printing May 1984**
**Third Printing August 1986**
**Fourth Printing August 1988**
**Fifth Printing January 1990**

Printed in U.S.A.

Library of Congress Catalog Number:
83-80395

ISBN 0-934706-09-3

# Foreword

For 30 years readers have been submitting ideas to Ceramics Monthly for publication in the Suggestions column, one of the most well-read departments in the magazine. Begun in 1953 as a periodical to serve the needs of the newly emerging studio potter, the magazine has grown along with the field, and now reaches an international audience of over 40,000 potters, ceramists, sculptors, teachers, students, ceramic historians and collectors.

As our file of Suggestions grew, subscribers began to tell us they wanted the best of these ideas in a more useful, accessible form—perhaps as a handbook. A pocket-size format was selected for its ease of use.

In deciding which of the 2500 submitted suggestions to publish, we had to determine if the idea presented was relevant, or if time had made the item obsolete (not too many wringer washers are readily available for conversion into slab rollers or slip mixers today, and only one suggestion utilizing this equipment remains). A few of the "helpful hints" presented here may seem obvious to experienced potters but prove revelations to others — it all depends on one's realm of experience. And while some may bring a smile, that serves a useful purpose, too.

Barbara Tipton
Associate Editor
*Ceramics Monthly*

# Table of Contents

**Clay Forming Processes** . . . . . . . . . . . . . . . . . . . . 1
    Clay . . . . . . . . . . . . . . . . . . . . . . . . . . . . . 2
    Handbuilding . . . . . . . . . . . . . . . . . . . . . . . . . 10
    Throwing . . . . . . . . . . . . . . . . . . . . . . . . . . . 21

**Clay Finishing Processes** . . . . . . . . . . . . . . . . . . . 31
    Decoration . . . . . . . . . . . . . . . . . . . . . . . . . . 32
    Drying and Finishing . . . . . . . . . . . . . . . . . . . . 38
    Glazes . . . . . . . . . . . . . . . . . . . . . . . . . . . . 42
    Glazing . . . . . . . . . . . . . . . . . . . . . . . . . . . 54
    Wax Resist . . . . . . . . . . . . . . . . . . . . . . . . . . 61
    Firing . . . . . . . . . . . . . . . . . . . . . . . . . . . . 64
    Troubleshooting . . . . . . . . . . . . . . . . . . . . . . . 72
    Fired Ware . . . . . . . . . . . . . . . . . . . . . . . . . 78

**Tools** . . . . . . . . . . . . . . . . . . . . . . . . . . . . . . . 81
    Tools for Throwing Processes . . . . . . . . . . . . . . . 82
    Tools for Hand Processes . . . . . . . . . . . . . . . . . 89
    Decorating Tools . . . . . . . . . . . . . . . . . . . . . . 96
    Mixing Tools . . . . . . . . . . . . . . . . . . . . . . . . 104

**The Studio** . . . . . . . . . . . . . . . . . . . . . . . . . . . 107
    Equipment . . . . . . . . . . . . . . . . . . . . . . . . . 108
    Kilns . . . . . . . . . . . . . . . . . . . . . . . . . . . . 122
    Plaster . . . . . . . . . . . . . . . . . . . . . . . . . . . 134
    Studio Operation . . . . . . . . . . . . . . . . . . . . . 141

**Appendix** . . . . . . . . . . . . . . . . . . . . . . . . . . . 150

# Section I

# Clay Forming Processes

# Clay

## Finding Clay

**A very detailed and accurate map of soil** types is available from the United States Department of Agriculture. With its help one can find areas where roads have been cut through clay layers. These outcroppings are readily accessible, and a top layer of dirt does not have to be removed.

**Try firing mud dauber nests** as a test and novelty; some found in barns contain too much humus to remain intact after bisque firing, but nests gathered from daubers who mined lake sites and creek bottoms often fire with great success. Clay from their digs has yielded a primitive but plastic body that fires a bright orange at Cone 10 and another which makes a green-gold Cone 10 glaze.

## Processing

**When mixing substantial quantities** of clay by hand, try combining the ingredients in a large cardboard box and blending the clay and feldspars with a garden rake. This can save time and wear on the hands, and the chance of breathing in the dust is reduced because you are mixing from a distance.

**Try drying large quantities of slip** in the pant legs of old blue jeans. Tie off the pant legs at the bottom and pour slip in up to the crotch. Fill both legs and sling the jeans over a tree branch. Hang until firm.

**To drain excess water** from clay slip, fasten pieces of untreated wet canvas to large containers with clothespins. Canning kettles, washtubs and dishpans may be purchased from Goodwill and the Salvation Army for this purpose. When the water has drained from the clay, remove the clay from the canvas, then wrap it and store it away until it is needed.

**For a steady supply of clay** here is a good way to mix your own from bagged dry clays (50–100 lb. bags). Order clay in bulk amounts, even if you need relatively small amounts at a time, because dry clay can be kept indefinitely with no special storage problems. Make a wooden frame to fit in some unused corner or floor space, and line the frame with a large sheet of plastic that allows plenty of overlap to cover later. Into the frame put dry clay powder and water in layers (such as a 2-inch layer of dry clay and wet this down, and add another layer of clay and wet it down). If mixing a clay body from several clays, spread clays together (dry), and wet down. If you are unable to guess how much water to use, tend to use too much, as it is easy to let it dry later. After wetting clay, cover tightly with plastic overlap and let it set for a few days. Then clay may be taken from the plastic and stored in covered containers. Then mix another batch of clay, thus keeping a container of clay ahead so the clay can age. This aged (for at least one week) clay, well-kneaded and wedged, is very satisfactory; there is no need for heavy equipment or tools.

**A child's rigid plastic swimming pool** works well for mixing dry clay. It's inexpensive, comes in large sizes, and the walls keep the dry clay from splashing out. Be careful to use a hoe with rounded corners, or one wrapped in plastic, so you don't puncture the pool when mixing.

## Reclaiming Clay

**To reconstitute clay from slurry:** stir the slurry to a smooth slip consistency with as few lumps as possible, then pour it into a strong cloth bag (such as an old army duffle bag). Tie or wire the bag tightly shut and place it on cement, preferably in the hot sun, for a few days. This method eliminates the need for large plaster drying bats, but is a little slower.

**In drying out slurry,** a hot sidewalk in place of a plaster drying bat works to perfection. It is particularly handy if you have large quantities of slip to dry out.

The procedure is merely to hose the sidewalk, making sure

it is clean and letting it dry. The slip is then poured out and in no time at all the excess water is absorbed. It is then a simple matter to peel off the large clay pancakes and wedge them for use. The underside will invariably dry more quickly than the topside so you might want to turn the clay over to give quicker and more even drying.

**Clay that has become too hard** for use may be softened by slicing into ½-inch slabs (or breaking into pieces), spraying with water and encasing in a pierced plastic bag. Put the package into a microwave oven for five minutes on high. The clay will be warm and thoroughly moist.

**An old canvas lawn chair** can be used to recycle clay. Extend the lounge until it becomes horizontal, pour slurry on it about 2 inches thick, cover it with an old sheet or canvas and let the clay drip-dry for two days. Remove, wedge and use.

**A simple yet time-conserving method** of recycling old dried scraps into fresh, usable clay is to line a wheelbarrow with a 4–6 mil polyethylene plastic sheet, on which is dumped a good amount of dried scraps. The openness of the wheelbarrow makes crushing the larger scraps a snap. They are then sprinkled with water or left outside in the rain. After a day to soak, the excess surface water is dumped off, the clay left to dry slightly, and finally the four corners of the polyethylene sheet are picked up and tied with wire to form a plastic bag for storing the clay. This procedure keeps dry clay storage to a minimum as well as providing a good supply of wet clay at all times. Small batches of fresh clay can also be mixed this way. A standard wheelbarrow is good for 300 pounds of clay, which can be moved about easily without the usual transfer from a mixer to a storage container.

**To remove lumps in clay** for recycling, place an old tennis racket in its press. The press sits well on the top of a small plastic garbage can or bucket, and its screws keep it in place.

Throw a piece of lumpy clay—about the size of a tennis ball or smaller—through the racket into the bucket. A lot of clay can quickly be reprocessed this way and will be almost as good as new.

**For reprocessing dry trimmings** and clay scraps, use an old meat grinder. It is convenient for small batches, and the process is dust-free. Clay dug from the ground and then dried out can also be put through the grinder for easier processing.

## Clay Storage

**An old, portable dishwasher** with the working parts removed makes an excellent, airtight cabinet for clay storage. Simply cover any holes with duct tape. The top-loading models work better; they are on casters and the top affords a good working surface.

**Try storing plastic clay** in the ground. Dig a 10-cubic-foot hole (large enough to hold a half ton), cover with a wooden lid, then roofing material. Clay stays moist indefinitely and it doesn't freeze in the winter.

**As a plastic bag of clay** is used up, dry flakes of clay form inside the bag and fall into the moist material. This nuisance can be completely eliminated if the clay first is placed in a cloth bag, then into the plastic.

**Line the inside** of clay storage cans with plastic trash bags. To reach that almost inaccessible last bit of clay, just remove the liner and turn it inside out.

**When storing plastic clay,** place pieces of strong plastic between layers of the body. Later, these sections may be easily removed in chunks instead of in handfuls.

**Moist, wedged clay** can be kept workable for years if you practice the following procedure. Place the clay in a plastic bag together with a moist, large-size cellulose sponge. (Do not use wet cloths instead of the sponge because they will rot.) Twist the top of the bag and place it upside down in another plastic bag. Twist the top of the outside bag and tie it with string, or fasten with a spring clothespin. Then place in an airtight container where it will stay moist and ready to use for years.

**To quickly identify** various bagged clays, tie the necks with short pieces of colored wire from inside telephone cables (obtained from Ma Bell or sometimes at the dump). These come in ten different colors, are flexible and rustproof. A mixture of clays receives a twist of two or more colors.

## Clay Additives

**Vermiculite in a clay body** gives an interesting colored and textured surface. It is particularly effective in a dark red-brown body, providing a contrast between the dark color of the body and the "gold fleck" of the vermiculite.

**An inexpensive and versatile substitute** for perlite in ceramic sculpture bodies is "popcorn" foam packaging materials. Particles of various sizes can be ground in a meat grinder. Because of the potential fume danger, be sure to fire these works in a well-ventilated kiln.

**Coffee grounds** wedged into clay burn out in the firing and can result in a pleasingly pitted body.

**When throwing porcelain,** add about ¼ cup white vinegar to the throwing water to keep the slurry in suspension, thus preventing feldspar from dropping out into a hard layer at the bottom of the bucket. The vinegar water is beneficial to the reclaimed scrap as well.

**To avoid the white film** on bisqueware caused by soluble salts, add 2½% barium carbonate to the dry mix clay.

**Adding 3% F-1 wollastonite** to many clay bodies can very often reduce or eliminate cracking, provided that the body is a good one and that the ware is not allowed to dry too quickly. This method is particularly useful for thrown plates and flat-surfaced ware in which cracking tends to be more frequent.

**If you live near a steel production plant,** you may be interested in using granular slag, which is an accessible waste product. As an addition to a Cone 10 clay body it gives either black metallic spots or grayish glazed spots. Finer particles will form spots, while pea-sized pieces will become fluid and run slightly. This material is not very good for ware designed for table use, but for larger ornamental forms, or for rough-looking planters, it is fine. When slag is wedged into clay it may be necessary to add some more water during the process.

## Grog

**To make grog,** grate a lump of plastic clay the consistency of cheese on an ordinary, fine, kitchen grater. Bisque fired in pots, it makes very uniform grog, eliminates screening and produces practically no dust.

**Save clay scraps** and trimmings from foot rims, let them dry thoroughly, then chop them in a blender to make grog. The resultant clay particles make an excellent grog after bisque firing. Porcelain grog and colored grog can also be made this way.

**To make grog,** use slip which is too dry to restore to casting consistency. Push through a window screen, dry, crush, fire and sieve to grade.

**For grog production,** roll out a thin sheet of clay and allow it to dry thoroughly. When it is dry, roll over it again, crushing the clay sheet into small particles, screen, then fire. It is much easier to first crush the clay, then fire it, instead of vice versa. Incidentally, the resulting grog particles will be quite smooth and easy to handle because this procedure produces very few sharp edges.

**Earthenware grog** can be made in the studio very easily by obtaining some soft, old, red bricks and breaking these into the particle size needed. First break the bricks into smaller chunks with a stout hammer, then put the chunks into a container such as an old iron kettle picked up at a second-hand store. For a pestle, use a heavy, rounded stone to pulverize the brick chunks.

**Floor sweepings** from a busy studio can often be used to make a variety of sizes of grog. After bisque firing the sweepings in a greenware bowl to burn out impurities and organic matter, screen them to the desired particle sizes.

**An inexpensive, coarse grog** can be bought at the supermarket in the form of cat litter. It is a little more absorbent than commercial grog; otherwise there is little difference.

**An inexpensive and universally available grog** for low-temperature (up to Cone 04) ware for raku or sawdust firing is industrial oil absorbent—a sweeping compound obtainable from automotive supply houses.

## Plasticizers

**To make new clay more plastic,** add one package of dry yeast to a gallon of water. Dissolve the yeast and add ⅔ cup of this mixture to 100 pounds of moist clay: poke deep holes in the clay with a dowel, then pour the water in the depressions, cover with plastic, let it stand several hours, then wedge, cover again and it will be ready for use within a day or two.

**To increase the plasticity** of any clay body, add unflavored, natural (not Swiss style) yogurt. Place the clay in the kiln area (for a little added heat), wait a week or two and the bacterial action will do the rest.

**If clay is too short,** wedge in a few drops of glycerin before working with it. It's surprising how much more plastic the clay will be.

**Bentonite can be added** by slicing moist clay in layers ¼ to ⅜ inch thick. Sift a uniform layer of bentonite onto the thin slabs, pile them together and let them set for two or three days wrapped in plastic. The bentonite absorbs the moisture from the clay and can be wedged in easily.

**Slowly sift dry bentonite** into a running blender containing a cup of water. The clay will reach the jelly stage in a few minutes, and after aging, seems more plastic and easier to use than conventionally mixed bentonite.

**If you recycle aluminum cans** and mix your own clay, keep a bucket of slip near the bags of empty cans. Before dumping a can, empty its last drops of liquid into the slip. That keeps the bag of cans drier and also helps age the slip before mixing with dry clay for pugging.

## Shrinkage

**To determine the percent** of shrinkage in a clay body, roll out a small slab slightly over 10 centimeters long. Press a plastic ruler (with raised numerals in inches on one edge and centimeters on the other) into the clay from 0 to 10 centimeters. Even backwards, the numbers can be read easily. Then fire the slab as usual. With the ruler, measure the amount that the 10-centimeter length has shrunk. If it is 1 centimeter shorter, then the amount of shrinkage is 10%, and so forth.

**To estimate the finished size** of a ceramic object after fired shrinkage (for instance, a 12-inch plate), first determine the percent of shrinkage for your clay—13% (0.13) is typical for porcelain. Subtract this from unity: $1.00 - 0.13 = 0.87$. Divide the shrinkage factor into the finished size you wish to obtain: $12 \div 0.87 = 13.79$. This answer is the diameter which must be thrown to end up with a 12-inch plate when using clay with 13% shrinkage. The formula applies to any dimension.

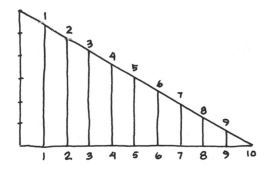

**Here is an easy way to make a ruler** for clays, which will tell you beforehand the size of any dimension after firing. Draw a right triangle (graph paper makes this easier) and mark off 10 units in an inch or centimeter scale on the horizontal side. (This scale represents the fired size.) Draw the vertical side with 6 units. With lines perpendicular to the horizontal scale line, project these inches or centimeters to the hypotenuse of the right triangle. These lines will intersect the hypotenuse, creating a new scale for the clay before shrinkage. This ruler reflects an average shrinkage rate of 14%, which is usually close enough for most clays.

# Handbuilding

## Building Techniques

**Waxed milk cartons** cut to size make excellent patterns for slab work. They do not wilt, are easily pulled off damp clay, and can be used a number of times.

**Perfectly shaped lids** and bases for oval casseroles may be produced using a guide made with simple geometric principles. Start by placing two pins at the center of a piece of paper. Put a loop of string around the pins and a pencil inside the loop. By moving the pins increasingly further apart and by experimenting with string length, a suitable shape may be drawn.

**A carpenter's square** or T-square is invaluable when cutting clay slabs to form the sides of a box or other rectangular form. If a ruler is used, the resulting pieces are not so true.

**When slab building ware,** a lot of time can be wasted waiting for the slabs to become leather-hard; but waiting time can be virtually eliminated by the use of a microwave oven to speed drying.
Roll out slabs on a small cloth, then slide the whole works into the microwave for one to three minutes. Include a partly filled cup of water to absorb some of the energy (and avoid possible damage to the oven). A couple thicknesses of newspaper underneath will absorb some of the moisture in the clay; a heavy book on top—separated from the slab with a layer of newspaper or a towel—will help eliminate warpage.
Turn the slabs over when cooling to allow for even drying.

**When drying handbuilt slab forms** that you wish to keep true—try placing blocks of wood on all four sides. Of course, heavy slabs of plaster also would be good if they are available. Leave the blocks with the object until the clay is dry. No more disappointments with warped sides. This same principle also applies when making tiles. To keep them from warping, dry between slabs of plaster or blocks of wood.

**After rolling out** ¼-inch or ⅜-inch slabs, use a long piece of threaded brass or iron rod as a thin rolling pin to groove one or both sides of the clay. The resultant texture tends to prevent curling corners and irregular drying.

**Instead of using a pair of sticks** for a thickness gauge when rolling out clay slabs, try using an old picture frame that is not very deep. Invert this frame on a piece of cloth, place the clay inside the frame and cover it with another piece of cloth, then roll away.

**You can make small slabs** of clay without following the usual rolling procedure. Merely place a damp cloth or wax paper on an ordinary commercial glazed tile (or any smooth surface), followed by the clay, another sheet of waxed paper or damp cloth, and finally another tile. Press the two tiles together with a horizontal twisting motion and the clay will gradually be forced into a smooth slab.

**An easy way to lift** large slabs, especially from a slab roller, is by rolling them around a rolling pin. This method allows minimal and consistent stretching, as well as easy maneuverability of the slab.

**Attaching sectional wheel-thrown forms** can be accomplished while they are quite wet. If the sections are not undercut when the bat is removed from the wheel, it is relatively easy to invert one still-wet pot and attach it to another freshly thrown form on the wheel.

**To save opening a jar** and washing a brush when joining pieces of clay, keep some slip in an old plastic squeeze glue bottle. After serrating the edges of the pieces, just squeeze the slip from the bottle onto the roughened parts and join. It doesn't spill and is always handy.

**For welding together parts** of a slab-built object, apply the necessary slip with a cake decorator. The selection of nozzles supplied with the decorator makes it easy to select the one that will give just the required amount of clay slip. Thickening the slip with epsom salts makes it easier to handle, by the way.

**When joining two clay pieces** together, some of the slip often oozes out. If it is in a hard-to-reach place, try using a small watercolor brush to wipe the excess slip away. The bristles don't damage the clay piece but do absorb the slip, and the brush is easily cleaned for further use.

**A wedge-shaped pencil eraser** fitted onto the handle of a needle tool works well for joining slabs or thrown sections. The rubber is soft and pliant like a small fingertip, but able to reach places the hand cannot.

**A small wooden wallpaper roller** removes the seam lines and finger marks on slab works while giving a smooth quality to the object.

**Roll a tennis ball** inside bowls or plates to form a smooth interior when handbuilding.

**When modeling plastic clay** on a banding wheel place a plastic bowl cover with the elastic edge over the wheel—the elastic pulling the cover tight. The clay working is then done on top of the plastic. When the work is completed, it is a simple matter to slip the cover from the wheel and peel it from the bottom of the form, eliminating the danger of marring the base.

**When working with handbuilt forms,** it can be difficult to determine if the ware has been trimmed exactly level. To clarify this problem, take a piece of glass (an old window pane will do), wipe it clean, then place it on the trimmed lip or foot. Through the glass you can get an exact picture of the clay surface, revealing whether further refinement is needed.

**To obtain a uniform height** for the walls of slab structures, just measure the height in a few areas around the pot and connect these points with a piece of string, circling the pot and holding the string in place, if needed, with pieces of clay. Draw a line around the container where the string lies, then cut the walls at the line and it should be the same height all around.

**A small plastic pill bottle** can be used to punch quantities of beads from a slab. Pressure inside the bottle ejects the clay plugs, which are pierced in the center with a plastic straw. Leatherworking stamps may effectively texture and decorate the surface.

**When making clay beads** for necklaces, string them on a piece of heavy monofilament fishing line available at most sporting goods stores. The line burns out when the beads are fired, leaving perfect holes for stringing.

**A quick and easy method** to make the stringing holes in ceramic beads is to slip small balls of clay onto sock knitting needles (these are pointed on both ends, and may be made of either steel or plastic), and then pinch them into the desired shapes. Place the needles across two sticks in the damp box and, when the beads are leather-hard, slip them off the needles for decoration. When they are dry, they are ready to glaze and fire.

**To make small-** and medium-sized beads take a walnut-sized piece of clay, form it into a short cylinder approximately the thickness of a cigar, and insert a plastic drinking straw lengthwise through the center. Roll the clay on a smooth surface until the desired diameter is achieved, then cut the cylinder into individual lengths with a razor blade or utility knife. The beads may now be pushed carefully off the straw, singly or in groups to be separated later. For larger beads, increase the diameter of the armature.

## Coil Building

**A simple coil-cutting tool** can be constructed very easily from heavy coat-hanger wire that is wrapped around an iron pipe of the desired coil size, then twisted with pliers several times for strength and stability. The remaining portion of the wire can be formed into a handle. To make coils, first form some soft clay into a rectangular block, the longer the better, then draw the coil cutter through the clay, just below the surface, in a straight line from one end of the block to the other. If the coils produced are not round, the cutter was not kept beneath the surface, or else it was not pulled through the clay in a straight line.

**Coils may be made easily** by using a regular large-sized meat grinder that clamps onto a table. Remove the metal plates and replace them with wooden ones (plywood is ideal) of the same thickness. Drill one center hole for them to fit on the grinder and make several dies, drilling holes of different sizes slightly below the center for various-sized coils. A hopper made from a plastic bleach or vinegar bottle and a round piece of wood to push the clay down make it easier to feed the grinder.

**To join coils** when handbuilding, make a V-shaped notch in one end of the coil and fit the other end into it (similar to a snake taking a bite of its own tail). Then smooth the joint with slip. It doesn't take as much time to do this as lapping over and smoothing out the hump.

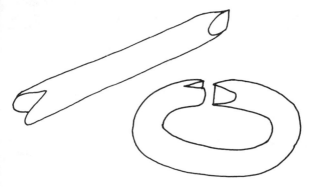

**To "foot" a coiled pot** simply roll clay to the thickness you wish to use for the base and cut out two pieces of the same size for the base. Place one thickness on the working surface and cover it completely, top and sides, with a piece of nylon. Next, place the other clay piece on top of the nylon-covered bottom section. Then proceed with building the wall with coils and place the first coil at the bottom of the lower base piece. When the pot is finished and has reached the leather-hard stage, the lower round and the nylon will lift out very easily and leave a very neat foot rim.

## Handbuilding Supports

**Elastic bandages** are ideal for wrapping large sculptural ceramics to provide support during drying, because the bandage shrinks with the clay. The flexible strips are available in lengths several yards long; the 2- and 3-inch widths are the most adaptable. Ends are easily secured by the accompanying metal clips.

**When a large coil** pot starts to slump, put a piece of cloth around it, pull the pot back into shape, and pin the cloth with straight pins. The cloth will hold the pot in place, take up the excess moisture, and can be left on until the pot dries.

**When building coil pots** large enough to sag, wrap socks around them for support. Fastening the socks with a safety pin allows variation in the amount of elastic tension.

**When a slab is shaped** by suspending or slinging it on a cloth "hammock" inside a box, it usually is difficult to fasten the cloth to the edges of the box. This is a particularly troublesome task because the cloth may need to be refastened several times until just the correct shape is obtained. Spring-type clothespins can be used for this task, and are much easier and quicker than thumb tacks or any other material.

**Balloons** can serve as molds for shaping objects made from slabs or coils, and can support oval or round clay shapes that show a tendency to sag as they are being built or as they are stiffening to the leather-hard stage. A blown-up balloon can be eased inside, or it can be partially inflated, placed inside, and then be inflated to the needed size. As soon as the clay can hold its shape, the balloon can be deflated and removed. This is a useful technique for handbuilding; perhaps it would work for wheel-thrown shapes also.

**Twisted lengths of newspaper** make excellent supports around the sides of "folded-up" shallow bowls. In making slab sculpture or other hollow forms, wadded-up newspaper stuffed inside keeps forms from collapsing—and readily burns out in bisque firing.

**To maneuver extremely thin slabs** of clay without tearing or otherwise distorting them, roll out the very thin slab on a piece of cheesecloth. The desired shape is made by running a knife or pointed tool through the clay, and the cheesecloth is cut with a pair of scissors. The thin slab of clay and the cheesecloth are then picked up together; in fact, they stay together even in the kiln.

This backing of cheesecloth keeps the slab intact and burns out in the kiln without any ill effects. Of course, it leaves its mark on the surface of the clay, making this method usable only where a textured surface would not be objectionable.

**When handbuilding a closed form** which requires rag or paper support inside, wrap the stuffing in a thin plastic sheet. Moisture will be forced outward rather than being absorbed by the stuffing, which may help prevent the ware from cracking in the kiln.

**When handbuilding** with extended sections or parts liable to crack and break during drying, build supports with dry sponges. They should give just enough as the clay shrinks.

**When making sculpture** that must be hollow, plastic bags are excellent as a core. They are softer and more flexible than paper bags, newspapers or paper towels, and of course they burn out during firing. Just roll out clay and wrap it around a wad of plastic bags. After the ends are joined to make a closed form, you can push and pound it into the shape you wish.

**To use cardboard cylinders** as forms for slab projects, such as vases, jars or even mugs, try wrapping the cardboard with aluminum foil, then proceed with the clay construction. The foil not only protects the cardboard and keeps it from getting soggy until the clay stiffens, but it also makes it easier to slip the cardboard cylinder out at the appropriate moment. The cardboard is removed when the clay will hold its shape but before much shrinkage takes place. Actually, other materials can be protected with foil in the same manner and utilized as mold forms: tin cans, glass jars, and even sewer tiles.

**Drinking straws** can be used most effectively as armatures for arms and legs when making small ceramic sculpture. Use the heavy-duty jumbo straws with "elbows" that bend; the clay can be built around these in almost any desirable position. The main advantage in using these is that you have a "built-in" air space that is indispensable in the drying and firing stages. Another advantage of using straws as armatures is that they will burn out in the firing and do not need to be removed.

**When making tall, slim sculpture**, cut a length of coat hanger and insert it through any part which needs support. Remove the wire as soon as the figure is dry enough to hold the weight or else the clay will crack; then plug the hole.

## Handbuilding Surfaces

**If clay sticks** to the roller when rolling out slabs, try using a piece of ordinary plastic on top of the clay. In addition to keeping your rolling device clean and the clay free of any unwanted texture, the plastic also allows you to "see through" and check the progress of the slab as you work.

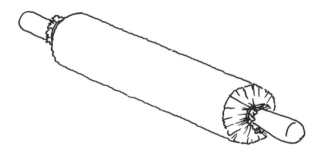

**If moist clay sticks** to your rolling pin when rolling out slabs, then cut one leg from a pair of old pantyhose, stuff your rolling pin into the leg, and tie it off at the handles.

**Nonwoven fabric** (the type used for linings and interfacings) makes a perfect surface for rolling clay, either by hand or slab roller, leaving no texture or markings of any kind. It comes in various widths and can be used repeatedly; the heaviest weight or thickness is best, as it will not stretch or wrinkle. It's available in discount fabric stores or can be acquired through clothing manufacturers in most areas.

**A strip of wax paper** makes a good surface for rolling slabs, and facilitates later transfer to the drying rack.

**Ceramists who use a slab roller** with a canvas-board bed may find slabs difficult to remove without stretching or bending the clay, which may lead to warping while drying and firing. To avoid this, use a piece of canvas cut ½ inch narrower than the board, and 2 feet longer. Fold 10 to 12 inches of canvas under the board, and slide it into the bed of the slab roller. Roll the slab as usual, pulling a little on the free end of the canvas to keep it straight and wrinkle free. Once the slab is made, put another board over the top and turn the slab over.

17

When the canvas is peeled back, the slab can be cut and removed without unwanted stretching.

This not only helps to cut down on warping, but with large volumes of work, the method saves time by allowing the slabs to stiffen elsewhere in the studio while further slab production can continue.

**As a replacement for canvas** or other handbuilding surface, cover the working area with new or used Wall-Tex wallpaper; the back side of the material is best.

**Save your old telephone books**—the sheets are a lot better than newspaper or paper towels for rolling out slabs and seem to shrink nicely with the clay. You never seem to run out of paper; a page will do in many cases, and if you need a larger size, just spread them out. The paper also works well between stacked slabs in storage.

**It is possible** to construct large sculpture for firing in a small kiln by working in sections without breaking the continuity of the building process. When the work is as high as the dimensions of the kiln will permit, spread ordinary kitchen plastic wrap across it and then continue building. The plastic paper clings to the clay and is thin enough not to cause a noticeable separation. Model the entire form in many sections and let them dry without moving them. When they are thoroughly air dry, lift the sections off and fire them separately. When cementing the pieces together after firing, they should fit perfectly.

**When forming clay** around an object such as a rock or a tube it is much easier to remove the clay if the form is first covered with plastic wrap. The plastic may be removed from the clay, or left to burn out during firing.

**Press molds,** used to obtain quick reproductions of forms for incorporation with thrown or handbuilt ware, become damp as the plaster absorbs water from the clay body. Soon the clay begins to stick to the plaster mold, resulting in distorted or damaged reproductions. Then the mold must often be set aside to air dry until it can be used again. Sawdust obtained from a lumber company mill shop sanding machine will remedy this. Before each impression is made, scoop some of this very fine sawdust into the mold and dump it out again. A fine film of sawdust will remain, enabling the clay to release instantly every time.

# Tiles

**To dry tiles successfully,** whether regular or irregular in shape, roll and cut them on a marble slab covered with oil-cloth, wrong side up. For drying, transfer the tiles to another marble slab covered like the first. Cover the tiles completely with blocks of wood about 2 inches thick. Check the tiles regularly, turning them over each day. Drying is slowed considerably, but tiles dry flat.

Tiles also are weighted in the bisque firing. Stack them flat in the kiln, one on top of the other in two or three layers. Place on top of each stack a piece of greenware large enough to cover the tiles, but not too heavy.

**If tiles tend to warp** during drying, try drying them between two plaster bats. If left between two very dry bats, they will dry out well enough overnight so that warping will be minimized and perhaps even eliminated completely.

**One of the handiest items** of studio equipment is a piece of smooth slate approximately a foot square. For making tiles or tesserae, roll the clay directly on the slate as thick as you want (even less than ¼ inch), cut the design through to the slate, lift off the excess clay, and allow the clay to rest a few hours on the slate. The tiles dry evenly with no warping or curling at the edges, and they slide off easily when they are leather hard. At this point place them flat under the slate for a day, while starting a new batch on top. The weight of the slate assures even tiles, and you never have to gouge out the backs to keep them from warping.

**To prevent irregular-shaped tiles** from warping during the drying process, place them on unglazed bisque tiles. Leave air spaces between the green tiles for more even drying. When a tile is full, put another bisque tile on top of the clay pieces. Then stack that tile with more forms, add another bisque tile, etc. When the last tile is in place on top, add a weight. All the clay tiles must be of the same thickness, of course.

**When making small tiles** for a mosaic, you can save a lot of time by glazing the rolled-out clay slabs with a single-fire recipe before the clay is cut into pieces. Simply roll out a slab of clay to the desired thickness, then apply the glaze heavily from a large brush. Allow clay and glaze to dry to the leather-hard stage where the clay can be cut without distortion.

**Styrofoam meat trays** from the local supermarket are excellent for drying slab and tile works, and objects don't stick to the surface. Filled and stacked four or five tall, they provide enough gentle pressure and air tightness to allow work to dry flat without special clay bodies. They do need to be rotated every few days to let all levels dry and prevent excess moisture from condensing on the bottoms.

## Molds

**A simple drape mold** can be made directly in clay and without the use of plaster. Simply form a slab to the desired shape and, when it is dry, bisque fire it. It will be porous, like plaster, and can be used over and over again.

**While drape molds** have been extensively used by the potter, and it is not uncommon to drape mold one plate over a previously fired form, the use of relatively stiff clay increases the efficiency of this production technique. When stiff slabs are used, the rim may be extended well beyond the supporting form and the clay tends not to adhere to the mold. When the new plate is leather-hard, a small coil may be added to the base of the plate as a foot rim.

**With a sheet of plastic** draped over its surface, a beanbag chair makes a versatile form for drape molding large bowls or platters.

**Cylinders of heavy cardboard** from 8 inches to 3 feet in diameter are available as scrap from companies that utilize them as molds for concrete pilings. They are waxed on the inside but untreated on the outside and are great as molds for forming slabs.

**Plaster press molds** for sprigging or tiles can be conveniently formed in a Pyrex pie plate. Use modeling clay to arrange the desired surface design on the interior of the plate; then pour plaster over the clay to an appropriate depth. Remove the completed mold by prying gently with a knife blade or screwdriver.

**For consistently better results** when casting ware, or parts for assembled forms, try warming the slip (about body temperature) before pouring.

# Throwing

## Throwing Techniques

**Place a mirror** in front of the wheel to reflect the wheel head. This is an invaluable aid when studying hand positions; it also makes it easier to compare them with photos when using a book as a guide. This process is also useful for viewing the pot as it is being made on the wheel, since it abolishes the necessity for the potter to step back to get a good view.

**Centering with eyes closed** is a useful teaching exercise for beginning potters. It helps them to recognize that centering is first a tactile and then a visual process.

**The following** is a rather uncivilized suggestion, but it works. When learning to throw on the potter's wheel, many are instructed to open with opposing thumbs. But with both thumbs in the hole, there is nowhere to hold a sponge. One solution is use your mouth, not to hold a sponge, but to hold a mouthful of water from a glass by your side. If you keep a steady stream aimed at the opening, it works beautifully. This method is probably not for demonstration purposes but, for opening large amounts of clay in the privacy of your own studio, it saves time.

**When throwing large pots,** hair-setting gel serves as an excellent lubricant which successfully burns out during firing.

**Many beginners have a tendency** to overwork the clay on the wheel (which is quite natural) and as a result the form collapses from being waterlogged. If a small bar of Ivory soap is finely flaked and kneaded into the clay, it will help prevent this waterlogging. Do not use Ivory Flakes or Ivory Snow because they are made to dissolve rapidly in water. The bar soap is made to withstand water and it is this quality that will help keep the clay from becoming waterlogged. The soap also acts as an added lubricant which helps you to throw without using too much water.

This technique is especially useful for throwing porcelain bodies (which are notoriously on the nonplastic side) because you can develop a thinner wall without the danger of collapse. Of course the pot must be bisque fired before a glaze can be applied—all of the soap will burn out in the kiln.

Use a small bar of soap to about 25 pounds of clay.

**Wedge a fair amount** of casting plaster into relatively wet clay shortly before using it; the plaster will continue to absorb moisture during throwing. This offsets the tendency of the clay to become wetter. As a result, the clay can be manipulated on the wheel for an extended length of time.

**When clay fatigue** is a problem for students learning to throw, use wallpaper paste instead of water to reduce absorption and softening of the clay body.

## Teapots

**Thrown teapot spouts** with cut lips are normally applied at an angle counterclockwise from table level to account for torque in the glaze firing. (When the pot comes out of the glaze kiln the spout is level and proper.) By throwing the spout on a wheel which reverses direction, this torque correction can be avoided. Throw half the spout with the wheel revolving in the normal counterclockwise direction and half the spout with the wheel turning clockwise. Alternate throwing in each direction, but start and finish in the normal counterclockwise manner. The spout may then be applied to the pot on the level, avoiding torque. For the experienced potter this skill may be accomplished in minutes.

**Those who experience** twisted teapot spouts after firing are pulling them up much too fast. It is possible to successfully fire untwisted spouts by throwing with fairly moderate speeds.

**To make S-shaped spouts** for teapots or other ware, throw an extra long spout and insert a length of plastic laboratory tubing when the shape has stiffened to soft leather-hard. The spout can then be modeled without collapsing or distorting the wall. Once the desired contour has been achieved, the clay should be allowed to set up somewhat before the tubing is removed.

**The answer to keeping spouts** in just the right condition for attaching is simply to put them inside the teapot and put the lid on until everything is ready—the teapot and spout both will be in the correct condition for completion.

**To keep the lid** on a teapot while pouring, the lid should be made with a straight flange to fit down into the rim of the pot. One side of the soft flange should be flattened, and—directly opposite—a small, V-shaped extension pulled. A corresponding flat edge, cut into the inside rim of the teapot nearest the spout, positions the lid correctly; while pouring, the V-shape will catch under the rim to hold the lid securely.

## Goblets

**To avoid off-center,** slanting goblets, throw them in two parts—the bowl, then the stem—and attach them when a little softer than leather-hard. Center and trim the bowl on the wheel, and with an old ball-point pen incise three concentric circles on its bottom. Use these as guides to attach the stem, and once it is centered, use a small bubble level to make sure the bottom of the foot is straight.

**When trimming the bowl** of a chalice before the foot is attached, leave a small knob in the center. It facilitates centering and sealing the stem to the bowl, lessening the chance of the pieces separating during firing.

**When throwing an addition** on a leather-hard pot, e.g., adding a stem to a goblet, cover the surface of the ware with thin plastic wrap, cutting a hole over the area where you are working. This keeps the remainder of the pot from absorbing excess slip and throwing lubricant which can cause cracking or deforming.

## Other Forms

**If pulling handles** is a mystery or if you are unhappy with the results, try throwing a cylinder, then cutting it in horizontal strips the width desired for the handles. These strips can then be attached in the normal way for pulled handles. The thickness and length will be determined by the size of the cylinder.

**Here is an easy,** fast way to produce hanging planters. Throw a fairly deep bowl, leaving the bottom approximately the same thickness as if it were to be footed; when the bowl is still soft, invert it, and center it on the wheel in the usual manner. Finding the center of the foot, poke a hole all the way through with your finger, and use the excess clay to throw a complementary drainage spout. Trim clay where needed, and add handles for hanging.

This technique is an improvement on the traditional upside-down throwing method, and consistently produces lighter forms.

**Large beads** may be efficiently and uniformly thrown on the wheel by pulling a narrow, vertical tube of clay about 4 inches in height. Then place a dowel into the center and use a needle tool to repeatedly slice through to the wood as the wheel turns. Remove the beads with the dowel, sliding each separately onto a bat. If formed with a minimum of water, the beads may be dried and fired quickly.

## Measuring

**Try using a metric ruler** for measuring the openings of jars, teapots, etc. It's much easier to get a good measurement in millimeters than in inches; just lay the ruler across the opening and record the figure for reference when making the lid for the ware.

**Inexpensive and time-saving devices** for repeatedly measuring uniform pot heights are a series of L-shaped shelf brackets which can be used like Japanese *tonbos*—the traditional form-sizing tools of the production potter. A 5-inch bracket may be perfect for goblet stems; a 4-inch bracket just right for mugs. This is more accurate and takes less time than using a ruler, and can't be accidentally moved like calipers.

**Use paint-stirring sticks,** marked in permanent ink with the height and width of the form, to measure the dimensions of production items such as pitchers, tumblers or mugs. Write the name of the item and the weight of the beginning lump of clay at the top. You can keep these sticks indefinitely, and use them instead of calipers to reproduce the approximate size of production ware.

**To quickly measure** equal amounts of clay for production throwing, center a large quantity of clay and proceed as if throwing off the hump. Instead of opening each centered portion, cut it free from the hump and set it aside, continuing the process until all the clay has been used.

**An easy way** to divide a pot into three equal segments for decorating is to use the top frame from an old lamp shade, which is a ring with three spokes running out from the center. Just place this in the center of any form you want to divide into three parts and mark off according to the spokes.

**To determine the exact placement** of three holes for hanging a planter, place a tripod stilt in the bottom of the pot. The stilt arms will point out the exact thirds of any object.

**To permanently and easily provide** a guide for holes or lugs for hanging planter rims or to key recentered pots on the wheel for footing, just file a small notch on the upper edge of the wheel head every 120°. Use a compass to find the equidistant notches by placing its point at the center of the wheel head and drawing a circle. Without changing the compass spacing, place the tip anywhere on the outline and intersect the circle (twice) with a drawn arc. Then place the tip at either intersection and swing a third mark. Use this as the center point for swinging another intersection. Lines can be drawn from the center of the wheel head through the three evenly spaced intersections to the rim for marking notch locations.

**To fabricate a tool** for determining the placement of holes in the rims of hanging planters, arrange three sticks (popsicle length or longer) at 120° angles and glue them to a small block of wood. This lightweight device can be rested on rims without distorting ware, and it is suitable for use on both large and small forms.

**Here is a simple way** to divide the rim of a pot into three equal parts. Take three soda straws the same length, run a string through them, then knot the string ends together. The resulting equilateral triangle can be placed on the rim of a pot and hole placement determined. Various lengths of straws can be used to make triangles for large and small ware.

25

**To divide a pot** into equal spaces for decorating with a re-peat motif, use a strip of paper about ¾-inch wide cut from the longest edge of a newspaper. Hold this around the area where the design is to be placed and pinch it tightly or fold it to mark the circumference. Cut the strip about 1 inch

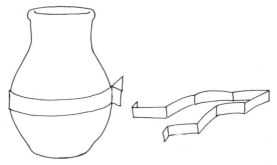

longer on each end for holding it. The space between these marks is then divided into halves, quarters or eighths—whatever is needed—and these marks are notched. The strip now is ready for use, and it is held around the pot and marked where the notches occur.

## Ware Removal

**When throwing** successively without a bat, wet pots often stick to the wheel head and are very difficult to remove even after being cut with fishline. This is made simple by dipping a sponge into water and squeezing the water on the wheel head, then cutting the pot from the wheel. Hold a bat or piece of wood at the edge of the wheel head and slide the pot easily and quickly onto the bat.

**When vertical shapes,** such as vases, coffee pots, etc., are removed from the wheel, they often become distorted at the rim because the clay is so soft and wet. To avoid this, a piece of newspaper can be placed on the rim and fastened to the clay by running a finger over it very gently at the point of contact with the clay. Air is trapped inside the shape, allowing it to be moved without any distortion.

**A couple of strips of newspaper** will aid in lifting a freshly thrown pot from the wheel head. The paper, applied to the sides of the pot, stops the hands from slipping, provides a more secure grasp, and limits the unwanted distortions that sometimes result when lifting a pot from the wheel.

**Rims of thrown bowls** often become distorted when they are removed from the wheel. Just before a bowl becomes leather-hard, turn it over on a flat surface and tap it gently. Because of the tension set up by throwing, the rim will resume its former shape naturally.

**Delicate shapes** thrown off the hump, such as spouts and goblet stems, can be removed from the wheel without warping if after the form is cut free, a "cookie" of clay is cut beneath the form and removed along with it.

**When throwing sets** of mugs or small pots, try removing the freshly thrown forms from the wheel head or throwing bat with a flexible knife rather than a wire. The knife causes much less distortion and the pots can be cut off, lifted and placed on the drying shelf in one motion, using the knife blade to support the wet pot as you move it.

To cut the pot from the wheel head, place the sharp edge of the blade alongside the base of the pot, flush with the wheel head or bat. With the wheel revolving very slowly, draw the knife toward the center of the base, thus freeing the pot. Without removing the blade, lift the pot with the knife and place it on the shelf, then slide the blade free.

**Use an old long-play record** to help get wide, low forms off the wheel; it's easy to slip under freshly cut ware.

**Large lids,** even though recently trimmed or with soft handles, may nevertheless be lifted without distortion by a strip of plastic sheet placed below the form. A few inches of plastic protruding on each side provide a grip for the potter, and the lid may even be lifted in this manner onto a pot flange for a size check.

# Trimming

**It isn't always necessary** to stick a pot down for trimming with wads of clay; the rim should naturally stick to a dampened wheel. A little practice will help you gauge how much water is necessary. After the pot is secure, place a bottle cap in the center, dampen a finger, and hold the pot down with gentle pressure while you trim the sides. Remove the bottle cap and trim the bottom. A sharp tap will knock the pot loose and you're ready for the next one.

**Fragile or textured rims** may easily be damaged while trimming the foot of a pot on a hard wheel head. By throwing a thin plate of clay on the head, a soft yet firm base into which a textured rim may sink is provided, thus lessening pressure on areas of relief.

**Prevent rim damage** to plates by trimming them on a bat covered with a ⅛-inch-thick piece of foam rubber.

**For miniature bottles** and other small items that are difficult and time-consuming to trim in the standard way, dampen one side of a large, flat, stiff sponge and attach it to the center of the potter's wheel with slip. As the wheel turns, hold the base of the pot firmly against the sponge. This produces a neat, even base in a fraction of the usual time. It works best if the pots are trimmed as soon as they can be safely handled, rather than waiting until they are completely leather-hard.

**After a bowl** has been trimmed on the wheel, it is often difficult to lift without losing its shape. To solve the problem, trim on a Masonite or plaster bat, remove the bat from the wheel head, place another bat on the foot rim and quickly turn the bowl upright between the two bats.

**To eliminate trimming** a foot on a thick-bottomed bottle, gauge its depth with a needle tool, then lay lath or board of the proper thickness to be trimmed on each side of the pot. Slide the cut-off wire along the wood in the same manner as cutting from the wheel head or a bat.

**Who has not cut** through the bottom of a pot when trimming the foot? The guesswork can be removed from trimming, along with the temptation of making the bottom just a trifle thinner, by premeasuring the exact thickness of the base. Hold a chopstick or dowel vertically next to the pot, sight across the lip, and mark the wood. Next place the stick in the pot and again mark the height. The distance between the marks represents the thickness of the bottom. Now the pot can be trimmed to the precise thickness desired.

**When trimming the base** of a pot, keep the wall about ¼ inch thick with the help of thumbtacks. Simply insert several into the wall from the inside of the pot so the point sticks outward into the wall. When trimming excess clay, the footing tool will hit the tack point when the proper wall thickness has been achieved. Remove the tacks and sponge the base lightly and the holes will easily disappear.

**A bat with an elevated** slotted head will enable trimming pots with high handles or other clay protrusions. Light vinyl padding may be added to the bat for protection, and also because clay adheres well to it. Another slot can be cut opposite the first if teapots with high spouts are required.

**A large, rather stiff brush** is just the thing for removing scraps of clay from freshly trimmed ware.

**That cheap little studio tool,** the needle mounted in a slender wooden handle or cork, is an indispensable gadget for reclaiming overly dry greenware pots.

Use it to incise areas that must be cut away for the foot rim whenever the drying clay tends to crumble or chip in the "bite" of the usual steel loop tool. Invert the form to be trimmed on the wheel head and mark the area that is to be retained for the foot. Next, incise the base with the sharp needle in a spiral design. After this is done, the loop tool can be used quite safely to cut into the brittle clay. This whole process can be repeated until the desired base treatment is achieved. Naturally, the drier the pot, the more care is necessary.

**An easy way** to make leather-hard-again ware without fear of cracking is to line the pot inside and out with wet newspaper, cover with plastic and leave it this way for a day; then it is ready for trimming.

**Potters can learn** to tap the base of a pot with the end of a finger, as physicians tap a patient's back. The sound will indicate the thickness. This percussion test can be repeated during the trimming process until the proper thickness is attained.

## Chucks

**Use earthenware planting pots** as chucks. They are inexpensive and come in graduated sizes. They also soak up moisture from the clay almost as well as a bat.

**Plastic foam flowerpots** generally make versatile chucks and may be found in a wide range of sizes in a nursery. They are soft, smooth and slightly flexible, easily adjustable to minor variations in contour, cause no damage to the clay surface, do not break if dropped and are one of the few lightweight things around a ceramics studio.

**Keep a supply** of trimming chucks—all greenware. To fasten, the rim is first dipped in water, then placed on the wheelhead and tapped to center. The slight amount of slip formed is enough to hold the chuck without additional clay.

**For a place** to put handle shapes until they are firm enough to attach, try throwing an hourglass-shaped, bottomless cylinder with a 2-inch outward roll on the top. After bisque firing, your chuck is ready to receive pulled, extruded or thrown handles around the top. Handles will be the same shape and curve every time, and the chuck can do double duty as a support for narrow-necked pot trimming.

**If you've had a bowl** with a rim larger than your wheel head you probably thought that you would need a large bat in order to trim the foot. Actually, any sized bowl can be trimmed if you first attach a trimming chuck or flower pot to the inside of the

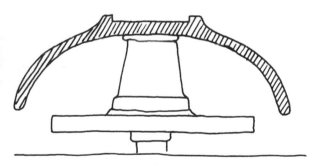

bowl with a coil of clay. The bowl is then inverted and rests on the chuck rather than on its own rim while being trimmed. If the chuck or prop used is tall enough, you can reach under and attach it to the wheel head. Also, a tall prop allows the bowl to clear the splash pan if this is necessary. If you throw your own trimming chucks, you can make some especially for bowls. Bisque chucks stick better if they are soaked in water before they are attached to the pots.

# Section II

# Clay
# Finishing
# Processes

# Decoration

## On-Clay Decoration

**Aluminum foil** is a very effective texture maker. Roll a slab of clay out over a rumpled piece of foil, or press the foil around a hand-molded piece while the clay is still quite soft. As the crinkles of the foil are pressed against the clay, it makes the initial pattern. As the clay dries, but before it becomes leather-hard, a loosely balled piece of foil can be twisted against this textured surface to deepen the pattern where desired.

**A simple but effective design** can be created on a draped form by stretching a coarse string mesh bag (such as the ones in which onions and potatoes are packaged) over the mold or the slab of clay. The clay should be firmly pressed over the mold for a clear design of the mesh. One advantage of using the mesh is that the clay can be left on the mold a little longer than usual since the string prevents cracking of the clay while drying, at least to a certain extent.

For an interesting variation, try soaking the string bag in underglaze and allowing this to become almost dry before placing it on the clay or mold.

**Rayon-type corded fringe,** in a 4–5 inch length rolled onto clay slabs, makes especially interesting patterns. Deeply textured terry bath towels and hand-crocheted rugs (old ones) are other sources for interesting textures.

**Place mats offer a variety** of interesting textures for impressing clay to be used for handbuilding.

**Old fiber glass curtains** can be cut into strips or shapes, dipped in an earthenware slip, and smoothed onto unfired ware. When fired to stoneware temperatures, the strips have a hard, slightly glossy surface which shows all the texture of the material. Some experimentation may be necessary, as a slip which is too fusible will cause the fiber glass texture to partially melt away; slip which is too refractory will give a dry surface. Good results have been obtained with a slip from local red clay maturing around 1150°C (Cone 02) to which is added 8% manganese dioxide and 1% cobalt, producing a semigloss black. A lower temperature red clay with no oxides fires to a red brown. The fiber glass can be cut on the straight grain or on the bias to drape more easily around difficult shapes. It can be applied to damp or dry clay, but unwanted smudges are easier to remove from damp ware. The material should be smoothed with the fingers to remove air bubbles and, if necessary, touched up with slip. It is easy to get an even application by laying the fiber glass on a nonabsorbent surface and painting the slip first on one side and then on the other.

**For figurative sculpture** that calls for realistic hair, try dipping pieces of horsehair or coarse dog hair into thick slip and applying it to the form. The hair burns out, leaving the exact hair shape and contour in clay.

**An interesting decorative effect** can be made by painting a design on leather-hard ware with some hot, liquid paraffin. (As soon as the decoration is painted, the brush may be cleaned immediately with carbon-tetrachloride until no trace of wax remains.) After the wax hardens on the greenware shape, a raised decoration can be made by rubbing away clay around the design, gently scouring with a damp, soft sponge. If there are signs that the wax is deteriorating, another application of wax can be made before continuing with the sponging action. The result of this technique is a relief decoration that appears to be carved.

## Slip Decoration

**Before using a slip trailer,** it is a good idea to bump the container end of the trailer on the table in order to rid the slip of any trapped air. When applying the slip, keep the tip of the trailer below the level of slip in the container end. By using these two precautions, you can maintain a more even feed.

**A three-color decorative effect** for low-fire work can be had by using two colored slips or engobes over a greenware shape.

Completely cover the greenware with a coating of a different colored slip, then put on another color of slip over the first. When a sgraffito line is cut through the slips to the body beneath, all three colors are revealed. By holding the sgraffito tool at an angle, or on the "bias," the bottom slip is revealed as a fine-line accent decoration between the mass of the surface slip and the broader line of body beneath. Any transparent glaze can be applied over this decoration.

**For an interesting effect,** mix black sand with slip and brush on leather-hard ware. Bisque fire, then glaze with either an opaque or a clear glaze.

**When you need a bit of slip** and don't want to blend and screen the entire pot of thick slip, stir it quickly, and add water to the top to obtain the right thickness. Then lay two thicknesses of nylon stocking on the diluted slip and dip a brush in the stocking "pocket." When finished, the stocking may be lifted out, rinsed or thrown away.

**If a batch of slip** accidentally has been mixed too thin, heat it in a pan until enough water evaporates to achieve the right consistency.

**Try mixing slip with glazes** — it's a great decorative effect.

## Underglaze Decoration

**Iron oxide wash** can be mixed with wax emulsion rather than water to achieve a more even application of the colorant. If an area gets too thick, it can be easily scraped thinner. When glaze is to be applied over the oxide designs, and the resist effect is not desired, the ware can be included in the next bisque firing to burn off the wax preliminary to glazing.

**Sketch patterns on unglazed ware** with red ink (never with blue) when in doubt about the way a design or decoration will look. The red ink burns out during firing, leaving no residue.

**If you apply glaze** directly over fresh underglaze without first firing, the decorative pattern can be kept from smearing if the surface is sprayed with any soft drink containing sugar. This technique also prevents smearing of airbrushed color.

**Decorate with copper wire** and glaze on a bisqued pot. Choose a shape which can be wrapped with fine copper wire (about 24 gauge) and fasten it securely by looping the ends together. Next, spray a glaze over the wire decoration and pot such as white or cream color gloss or semigloss. After firing to Cone 04, the wire melts and blends with the glaze to produce a textured green decoration against a light glaze background.

**A tennis ball** dipped in a wash of ceramic oxide colorants may be rolled over ware freely or with the palm of the hand to create a bold, expressive line. The nap of the ball acts like a paint roller, dispensing a steady colorant supply.

**For large, spontaneous strokes** of color, try oxide solutions in empty shoe polish bottles equipped with square foam applicators. The oxides can be stamped or stroked onto green or bisqueware.

**To transfer a design** onto clay, make a drawing on white tissue paper (the kind used for wrapping gifts) with a felt-tipped pen; when the paper is laid on the damp pot its water absorbs ink from the design. The tissue may be carefully removed for a second transfer.

## On-Glaze Decoration

**Try dipping a length of string** into a colored glaze and then arranging it on a bisqued plate, shallow bowl, or tile that has been covered with an opaque white glaze. When the ware is fired, the string burns away, leaving a glaze pattern in its place. String and cord of different sizes can be used, and more variety can be had by tying loops or knots in the string before it is dipped into the wet glaze.

**Flakes of dry glaze** will produce interesting patterns, including halos, when melted on flat glazed surfaces.

**Metal filings** such as copper, iron or brass can be fired over a glaze; when used individually or in combination, the results may be quite beautiful.

There are several ways of applying the filings. For smaller ware the design may be spread out on soft tissue with a fine brush and toothpick; while the glazed pot is still slightly damp, gently press it on the paper. If any paper adheres, just let it burn off in the kiln. Larger free-formed designs may be created by using a small rubber syringe available at any drugstore. The fine powder residue of the filings can be picked up easily with a straight-ended eye-dropper, and puffed on.

**Fill an empty baby powder container** with bronze or copper powder, and sprinkle this onto wet or dry, freshly glazed ware for a delicately speckled pattern after firing. These materials, available from metal fabricators or some ceramic suppliers, will fire green in oxidation, and red or gold in reduction.

**For a "different" glaze effect,** combine 1 teaspoon each of dry copper oxide, cobalt and iron and place the mix in a salt shaker. Sprinkle over any light-colored glaze for an unusual effect of small dots of green, blue and dark red. The "mix" must be applied on vertical surfaces while the glaze still is wet, but it can go on dry glaze on horizontal shapes such as plates, trays and tiles.

## Miscellaneous Decorative Techniques

**Run a motorized wire brush** over the surface of a glazed pot to leave an iron-gray deposit, then fire the ware to Cone

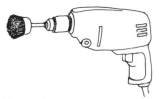

018 as you would any other luster glaze. After cooling, you will find that the deposit has formed a "rust luster." For a deeper brown color, fire to bisque temperatures.

**Glass beads** make interesting overglaze patterns and effects on the surface of platters or other horizontal ware. Glass may be high or low fired, and particularly unusual results occur in the stoneware range.

**For an effect** similar to raku crackle lines, apply thin china paint to crazed, glaze-fired ware, smearing it around a little before completely wiping it off with turpentine and paper towels. Fire to the appropriate cone. Matt glazes can produce interesting effects, and the crackle lines may be any color for which china paint is available.

**Try mixing dry glaze** with any oily or waxy substance for decorative application. The mix will resist other wet glaze—a good way to use two incompatible recipes successfully.

**For random-color results** in fired ware, try using a single-fire glaze instead of water or slip when throwing. Open the form using water, but substitute single-fire glaze to shape the pot. Surprising effects may happen, especially along the throwing ridges.

**Elmer's glue** applied full strength to bisqueware will cause those areas to reduce black in an oxidation sawdust firing.

**For a spill effect inside bowls,** dampen the ware and quickly apply a heavy coat of glycerin so that it puddles in the bottom. While it is still wet, dribble and pour thinned underglazes, engobes or glazes around the rim letting them flow into a marble pattern, or center the ware on your banding wheel and quickly cover the surface with glycerin. Spin the wheel and apply bands of various colors on the surface. Be certain to cover yourself and the work area, as the glaze flies. Once glycerin dries it is quite difficult to remove, but it fires off the ware without affecting the body or glaze.

**A rather interesting glaze effect** was achieved by accident: A bisqued pot was dipped in a glaze and then a design wax resisted over the glaze. After a change of mind about color, the glaze was removed. Everything washed off except where the wax had been used, so the wax and glaze under it remained in a perfect design. After firing, the effect was much better than if a design had simply been painted on the bisqued form.

**The right placement** of freehand brushwork can be difficult on concave or convex surfaces, especially when painting with oxides on glazed, unfired ware. To eliminate errors in placement, do a trial decoration on the pot using diluted India ink, then go over it with oxide or glaze colors. The ink will burn away with no trace, but be sure to use a clean brush, since even a trace of some oxides in the trial design may show up after firing.

# Drying and Finishing

## Drying Objects

**Two-inch-thick Styrofoam slabs** (the type used for insulation) provide an excellent surface for drying pots. Cut grooves into them an inch apart with a knife or wood-burning tool so air can get underneath the ware for better drying. Holes may be cut into the Styrofoam surface to support bottles for upside-down drying.

**Worn-out auto seat pads** can be a welcome aid in the studio. Discard the fiber covering and save the flat metal springs. Greenware placed on them dries faster and more uniformly since air can circulate around the bottom of the forms; also, hot pots fresh from the kiln can be set on them to cool without danger of burning wooden shelves.

**Dry clay objects on plaster board** (wall board). It cuts easily to any size and shape, and cleans with just a damp cloth. Portable shelves can be made by using sheets of this material with blocks of wood in between.

**An infrared bulb** can be a useful and inexpensive addition to the workshop. Like the sun, it dries objects from the inside out. Set it about 3 feet from your drying shelf and use it for speeding up drying of heavy clay works. (Don't let them get too hot.) It is also useful for warming glazed forms before reglazing, as the new application of glaze is easier.

**During exceptionally humid weather,** hasten the drying of greenware by placing the objects in a home gas oven with only the pilot light burning. Overnight the greenware should be thoroughly dried and may be fired as usual.

**To hasten drying** of greenware, use a hair blower/dryer.

**To allow for better air circulation** completely around a clay object as it dries, set it on two or more wooden tongue depressors. These will elevate a form just enough to provide faster and safer drying.

**When drying forms** with narrow tops which cannot be safely turned upside down, it is helpful to seal the top closed immediately after throwing. Cut a small piece of writing paper slightly larger than the pot opening, wet the paper thoroughly on both sides, and press it gently into contact with the rim of the opening.

**If rapid drying is causing cracks** in your ware, try rubbing a thin coat of motor oil on trouble-prone areas to retard evaporation. It does not leave a residue after firing.

**Large plates, platters** and other wide, shallow forms, whether thrown or cast in a mold, usually warp upon drying unless some type of frame or brace can be placed across their tops. This problem is especially acute with dinner plates measuring from 9 to 12 inches in diameter, which might not successfully be dried upside down because of sagging. Discarded panes of glass are the almost-perfect weight and density to allow uniform drying of all plates. Irregular edges and sharp corners should be slightly sanded or ground down for safer handling, or can even be covered with tape.

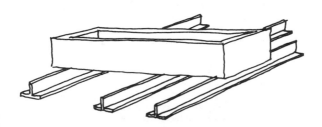

**The metal strips** that support acoustic tiles in suspended ceilings have a T-shaped cross section, and are available in approximately 4-foot lengths. Several of these may be spaced to support large slab or thrown forms for drying.

**During drying,** place plates or large, flat-bottomed pots across two kiln stilts laid on their sides and separated a little. This allows the bottoms to dry more evenly and helps eliminate cracking.

**To insure even drying** of freshly thrown pots, use egg separators from crates of eggs. These are about 11 inches square, and the raised portions permit the air to get under the pots which are set on them. The separators can be obtained from most markets where eggs are purchased in large quantities.

**If a plastic sheet** is used to cover wet pottery, it often mars or warps the ware. Instead, attach strings above the drying table and clip the plastic sheet to the string with clothespins so it does not make contact with the forms.

**To test** whether or not greenware is dry enough to go into the kiln, hold the bottom of the form to a cool window (one in the shade), and leave it there for about a minute. If there is a ring of moisture on the window pane then the clay isn't completely dry yet.

## Dry-Finishing Ware

**The edge of a fired cone** makes an efficient burnisher for polishing greenware.

**For a nonscratching foot rim** without adding glue, liquid rubber or other synthetic materials, burnish the foot with a spoon or other smooth object when the clay is leather-hard. After firing, any remaining rough areas can be smoothed completely with emery paper.

**After trimming a foot rim,** try burnishing the contact surface first with a small hardwood tool, then with a finger. This is similar to troweling concrete to submerge coarse grains and bring fine grains to the surface. Any roughness left after glaze firing is easily removed with a common household whetstone.

**After trimming the foot** of a heavily grogged object, brush the surface with matching slip to provide a smooth finish and afford protection for table tops and other contact surfaces.

**Fine steel wool** will smooth rough areas of greenware.

**When smoothing porcelain greenware,** use a fine-mesh plastic scrubbing cloth or pad (the type found in supermarkets and used to clean cookware) to avoid the iron contamination that often results from using steel wool.

**Flat, thrown lids** that do not fit can be smoothly and easily reduced in diameter with a steel wool pad. This method works better than using sandpaper, and won't chip the ware.

**Cotton net** (as in an old petticoat) makes a good smoothing material for rough spots or for removing the fin caused by a mold joint. It does not leave a polished look, get clogged or wear out, so it is economical and preferable to sandpaper.

**For fine-finishing greenware,** just ball up a piece of old pantyhose and use it as an abrasive scouring pad.

**An emery board** works well for sanding down small, extraneous pieces of clay from bisqueware. It fits comfortably into small areas where other sanding devices—sandpaper, steel wool, etc.—are too large. The board can also be cut down to sand even tinier places.

**To trim dried ware** with broad, flat surfaces, tape a sheet of coarse sandpaper to the wheel head, which then becomes a functional sanding disc. This is most effective for forms that are slightly drier than leather-hard, since wetter clay clogs the sandpaper more rapidly.

**Center an oversized lid** (leather-hard) in a chuck on the wheel, and gently but firmly hold a piece of metal window screen against the rotating form to trim an oversized diameter. The screening works better than sandpaper because it won't clog with clay.

**Heavy canvas** may be used instead of sandpaper for leveling the bottom of your ware. Place the canvas on a flat surface, tacking it down at the corners, if necessary. Then rotate the bottom of your dry greenware on it until it is level.

**Old glaze strainers** or sieves work well for smoothing the bottom of a greenware pot left to dry on a marred plaster bat.

# Glazes

## Mixing Glazes

**For removing excess water** from glaze when there isn't enough time to allow the glaze to settle and pour off the excess liquid, take three or four thicknesses of newspaper and depress these into a large mixing bowl. Next, pour the glaze into the center of the paper. The water will be absorbed into the paper and the glaze will remain on top. Now, just pour the thickened glaze back into its container and, with a rubber spatula, gently scrape off the glaze which had built up on the paper and return it to the thickened glaze. The whole process takes just a few minutes.

**When weighing large glaze batches,** the use of a typical potter's scale is very time consuming because the volume of various glaze compounds sometimes exceeds the capacity of the scale, and more than one weighing must be made. To solve this problem, mark a clear plastic bucket with the volume level of the larger quantities of material used in glaze batches. Each level also is marked with the glaze name and number for quick identification. One bucket can be marked with the volume levels of glaze ingredients for many glazes. Each glaze compound needed is poured into the bucket and vibrated gently until flat across the top. Then the volume can be determined. Colorants and other glaze compounds used in small amounts are still weighed in the conventional manner for accuracy. There seems to be no significant difference in formulas with this method of formulation, and it saves time.

**For a fast, efficient way to weigh and mix** test glazes, first weigh out 100–200 grams of the base glaze. Next, take plastic sandwich bags, label them with masking tape, and set the balance to the weight of the test sample you are going to work with. Ten or twenty samples of the base can be quickly placed in each bag, and percentages of oxides, clay or other chemicals may be added as needed. The samples can then be stored until needed, or water added right to the bags and mixed. Cut the corner of the mixed test glaze bag and pour what you need on tiles for glaze testing.

**The easy and safe way** to mix glaze is to put the dry ingredients in a plastic container and roll or shake to mix. Carefully pour the dry glaze into water and allow it to slake; an hour later it's dissolved without stirring.

**Mix small quantities of glaze** or slip in a coffee can with a plastic lid which has been perforated to accommodate a metal paint stirrer attachment for an electric drill. This apparatus works quickly and thoroughly, and the plastic cover prevents any liquid from splashing out.

**Dry mix glazes safely** and cleanly in a plastic bucket with a tight-fitting lid, such as those obtained from pastry or fast-food establishments. Through the center of the lid, drill a hole the same diameter as the shaft of your electric drill paint mixer, and for flexibility cut a small X through the hole. Place the dry ingredients in the bucket, insert the paint mixer through the lid, close tightly and mix. When the dust settles, water may be added (through an optional corked hole in the lid) and the glaze mixed to sufficient consistency for pouring, dipping or spraying.

**To prevent sticking** of the dry glaze ingredients to implements used in measuring, coat spoons, gram scale trays, containers or other utensils with silicone spray. After thorough drying, powders will slide easily, improving accuracy.

**When sieving wet glazes,** instead of assisting the batch through the screen with a hand or spatula, use a folded or rolled nylon net bag—the type onions come in—to rub over the sieve. The glaze seems to "fall" through in record time.

**The best way** to get bentonite dispersed in a glaze is to boil it (about 30 grams of bentonite in a pint of water), and then "blend" it (in the kitchen blender) for a few seconds. This amount works very well for a gallon of glaze.

**A hydrometer** for checking the specific gravity (density) of glazes and slips is easily made and costs nothing. In one end of an ordinary plastic drinking straw, insert a snug-fitting piece of steel rod—¼-inch diameter; a 1-inch length of welding rod fits perfectly in a McDonald's straw. Drop the heavy end of the straw into a slip or glaze that you will want to duplicate and mark the liquid level on the straw with masking tape. You can make a straw for each density you wish to record.

**When a glaze** is at its proper specific gravity, take a wooden dowel of any diameter and 6 inches in length, and put a screw in one end. Place the dowel in a container of glaze, screw-end-down; some of the dowel will be immersed, and the rest will stand perpendicular above the surface. Make a mark at the point where the dowel shows above the glaze, and use this to approximate the specific gravity of your next batch.

**A simple, but accurate way** of finding the density of liquid glaze is based on Archimedes's principle—density of a liquid equals weight divided by volume. One hundred cubic centimeters of water placed on a scale weighs 100 grams; when these two amounts are placed in the formula (100cc/100 grams = 1.0), the water's density equals 1.0. (Camera shops and scientific supply houses sell graduated cylinders and flasks suitable for measuring volume in cubic centimeters.) To ascertain the density of a glaze, stir and pour out exactly 100 cubic centimeters and weigh that amount, then divide the gram weight by the 100 cubic centimeter volume. Most glazes should have a density of 1.2–1.5 for dipping, and 1.5–1.8 for brushing. This technique is more accurate and convenient than a hydrometer, which requires a large volume of liquid before it will float.

## Glaze Storage

**When storing glaze** or slip in gallon plastic jugs, drop a handful of marbles into the liquid. Later when glaze is needed, the capped jug is shaken and the marbles quickly loosen and help dissolve all the settled glaze.

**A good supplier** of glass or plastic gallon jars for slip and glaze storage is a school cafeteria. Since these jars are usually thrown away, it seems most school-lunch-program cooks would be glad to give their empty jars to anyone.

**For airtight plastic containers** to store chemicals or glazes, inquire at a fish market about empty fish-shipping tubs. They hold about 2 gallons of liquid and are wide enough (about 12 inches in diameter) for dip-glazing bowls and shallow forms.

**To prevent glass** slip and glaze storage jars being broken from handling, put bumpers on them—2-inch bands cut from inner tubes.

**Eight-ounce plastic yogurt cartons** make ideal storage containers for 100-gram batches of glaze.

**To avoid** runny glazes ruining shelves and pots, mark all containers of very fluid glazes with a band of red tape. Now, if you forget that a previously mixed glaze runs excessively, the red tape serves as a warning to take the proper steps to avoid fusing the pot to the kiln shelf.

**If you store batches** of slip or glaze in wide-mouthed jars and have trouble with sticking screw caps, paint the threads with liquid green soap. This makes it possible to tightly cap the jar without introducing the problem of sticking lids.

## Reclaiming Glaze

**If glaze dries out** into a hard cake, slowly add any carbonated soft drink and stir. This mixes faster and smoother than water and it does not affect the end result.

**When spraying glaze** place the pot on a plaster bat. Excess glaze will be absorbed by the plaster instead of dripping off the base of the pot. When glazing is complete, the glaze can be scraped off the bat and mixed with water again.

**To catch overspray** in your spray booth, drape a sheet of plastic behind and underneath the object being sprayed. The overspray will cling to this background; when it is dry it is very easily brushed down, picked up and remixed with water.

## Raw Materials

**When a thick mixture** of manganese dioxide and water is applied to bisque or greenware, and fired to Cone 6, a metallic glazelike finish results.

**If bags of borax,** zinc or other chemicals have become rocky because of moisture absorption, a rolling pin and a flat, laminated board should pulverize these chemicals quicker than a mortar and pestle.

**When a glaze recipe** calls for borax or soda ash, boil these ingredients first in a little water until they are entirely dissolved, then add this solution to the wet glaze batch, and sieve.

If borax recrystallizes in a wet glaze during storage, sieve the crystals out, add hot water and boil again—use an enameled pan since these soluble materials seem to corrode metal. When the crystals are dissolved, add the solution back into the glaze and sieve.

**Glycerin, a syrupy liquid** available at most drugstores, has numerous uses in the studio. It lets glazes and slips flow more easily and helps bind them to the ware. Add a small amount of the following solution to glazes: 5% gum arabic, 50% glycerin, and 45% water.

**Local clay** may be better used as a glaze or glaze component. One recent batch threw nicely, but had so many calcium impurities, the spitouts were a problem, and the body cracked during firing. But this same clay made a beautiful rich, olive-gold glaze without further additions when fired to Cone 10.

**Small amounts of epsom salts** (approximately 1 or 2 tablespoons to 20 pounds of glaze) keep glaze particles in suspension, thus avoiding the rock-hard lump that collects at the bottom of the bucket.

**Three tablespoons dry** CMC gum mixed with 2 cups rubbing alcohol will cure swollen colemanite (or Gerstley borate) glazes instantly.

## Glaze Recipes

**A popular glaze** has been the simple wide-range formula: plastic vitrox 1, Gerstley borate 1, which is often made in a batch of 40 parts plastic vitrox to 40 parts Gerstley borate with 5 parts rutile and 5 parts Opax (or 5 parts tin) added.

Since plastic vitrox (PVC) is sporadic in availability, try substituting the following recipe: Pumice 43.6 parts, Gerstley borate 43.8, Edgar Plastic Kaolin 6.8, Flint 5.6. This formula is empirically similar, which explains the sameness of result. The increased iron from pumice might affect some colorants. Use rutile as a modifier and the difference is not detectable. This glaze can be put on a little thinner than the PVC glaze and is less prone to cracking in the raw state. The weights can be rounded off a good bit, too.

This recipe will endure practically any firing conditions including stuck temperatures, oxidation, any degree of reduction, and will be smooth and hard from a very soft Cone 3 to a very flat Cone 8, except when fired on a very dark body.

**As energy** becomes more of a concern to potters, more of them may be working in the Cone 4–6 range. A recent survey of 44 mid-range glazes—primarily reduction but suitable for oxidation as well—reveals two basic recipes that could be used as guides for experimentation.

Nepheline Syenite Glaze
(Cone 4–6, oxidation or reduction)

| | | |
|---|---|---|
| Whiting and/or Dolomite | 13% | (plus or minus 5%) |
| Nepheline Syenite | 47 | (plus or minus 6%) |
| Kaolin and/or Ball Clay | 7 | (plus or minus 2%) |
| Flint | 25 | (plus or minus 5%) |
| | 92% | |

Fill out the recipe with other fluxes (lithium, boron, etc.), or any flux-containing ingredient to arrive at 100%.

Feldspar Glaze
(Cone 4–6, oxidation or reduction)

| | | |
|---|---|---|
| Barium Carbonate | 12% | (plus or minus 4%) |
| Whiting and/or Dolomite | 10 | (plus or minus 5%) |
| Any Feldspar | 42 | (plus or minus 8%) |
| Any Kaolin and/or Ball Clay | 9 | (plus or minus 3%) |
| Flint | 19 | (plus or minus 6%) |
| | 92% | |

Fill out the recipe with other fluxes or any flux-containing ingredient to arrive at 100%.

In feldspar-based glazes, the following should be considered general guidelines: If the feldspar is increased above 50%, then the flint should be decreased 4%; if the feldspar is decreased below 35%, then the flint should be increased 3%.

**Transparent cobalt glazes** over a red clay body produce black. It is believed that the Early American pottery called "Jet Ware" was made in this manner. A light blue decoration may be produced with only a white slip on the red body before cobalt glazing. Firing reduction should ensure the black color.

**The ash residue** of charcoal briquettes used in outdoor grills makes a stable glaze ingredient. Sift the ash through an ordinary kitchen sieve three times, and incorporate it in the following recipe: 40 parts ash, 40 parts potash feldspar, 20 parts kaolin, and 15 parts whiting. Fired to Cone 6 oxidation, this glaze should produce consistently good effects.

**Here are two** simple Cone 6 oxidation glaze formulas employing Mount Saint Helens volcanic ash:

### Volcanic Ash Glaze I (Cone 6)

| | |
|---|---|
| Volcanic Ash | 75% |
| Wood Ash | 25 |
| | 100% |

### Volcanic Ash Glaze II (Cone 6)

| | |
|---|---|
| Volcanic Ash | 87% |
| Whiting | 13 |
| | 100% |
| Add: Zinc Oxide | 9% |

**You can step up** the red tones of a low-fire red clay body when covering with a clear glaze. Just add approximately 1% iron rust to the glaze batch.

**An interesting combination** of raku materials and techniques creates effects similar to those of certain types of salt-glazed ware, but without the use of salt. Use the following clay body:

### Raku Clay Body

| | |
|---|---|
| A.P. Green Fireclay | 20 parts |
| Calvert Clay | 7 |
| Cedar Heights Goldart Clay | 20 |
| Tennessee Ball Clay | 10 |
| Fine Grog | 30 |

The pots are bisque fired and then glazed with the following formula:

### Fake Salt Raku Glaze

| | |
|---|---|
| Borax | 25% |
| Frit 3124 (Ferro) | 75 |
| | 100% |
| Add: Bentonite | 5% |

Allow the ware to completely dry, and preheat your fuel-burning kiln to Cone 012. Load your kiln in the usual raku manner, but then close the damper until you develop a good reduction atmosphere. Maintain this atmosphere until the glaze melts, then open the damper and allow the kiln to cool for about five minutes before removing the ware. Reduction in the kiln will soften usually bright raku colors without leaving scars from glaze contact with leaves and straw.

## Glaze Binders

**Sugar-sweetened soft drinks** sprayed over airbrushed colors on pots keep the colors from smearing; they also protect oxide and slip applications when glazing once-fire work.

**Artists' matt acrylic medium** mixed into glaze provides a tough, inorganic binder.

**Liquid starch** makes an excellent glaze binder. It is easily obtained at any grocery and no mixing is required. Simply add it to the glaze. Once applied to bisqueware, the glaze dries to a very hard surface.

**Corn syrup** added in the proportion of about 1 tablespoon per quart of liquid glaze will allow glazed ware to be handled without fingerprints or chipping. The syrup tends to thin the glaze so use a smaller amount of water when mixing the glaze batch. If the glaze is to be stored, a drop of carbolic acid will act as a preservative and prevent fermentation.

**Substituting cornstarch** for gum tragacanth in glazes works well if you have to reglaze a pot. Mix the glaze thicker than usual, add enough cornstarch to make the glaze mixture even thicker, then apply to a heated pot.

**Sprayed glazes** (especially those applied with an atomizer) are usually left with a powdery surface that is easily abraded by handling. By lightly spraying the finished pot with a coat of very dilute wax resist (an ounce to a quart of water), a surprisingly durable surface can be achieved.

## Glaze Tests

**For those involved in glaze mixing** with frustrating results, analyze the mineral content of the water being used. A change in water can be very damaging, or it might give a whole new approach to a glaze which changes from smooth, semimatt to dry, pitted matt suitable for sculpture instead of a bowl.

**When testing glazes,** it may be helpful to mix a small batch of suitable proportion and then measure ¼-cup amounts into ten individual paper cups. Next, using plastic measuring spoons, add ¼ teaspoon of various oxide colorants to the ten test batches; with cobalt, halve the amount because it is such a strong colorant; with iron, double the amount because it is so weak. This ratio of ¼ cup glaze to ¼ teaspoon colorant closely approximates the ratio recommended by most books, and it is certainly a lot easier than figuring out the grams for each recipe. This is not an exact way of working, but it gives enough of an idea of how the colorants perform so that you know whether or not you want to test the glaze on a pot. And, you can check a number of glazes rapidly using this method.

**There are many variables** in acquiring satisfactory glaze results beginning with the source of the glaze ingredients; even a good supply company's materials will differ from time to time. Very precise weighing is a must. Calcining is also an important factor often overlooked and this alone can make a real difference. Location of the glazed item in the kiln and the variation of firing temperatures may be critical too. The length of the bisque firing and the cleaning and dampening of the bisque before glazing are also factors.

Adjustment is often the secret. Add or subtract frit, for instance, for more or less melting and fluidity (respectively) if the glaze lacks maturity. Or add clay or flint to adjust the glaze to a higher firing temperature and to reduce fluidity.

One method of testing a given recipe is to weigh 100 grams of the dry base glaze, divide this into five 20-gram portions, and place each in a small plastic bag or jar. Then add to these portions in 5% increments—measuring 1 gram is tedious but can be simplified by using a small piece of creased paper instead of a bowl. As a starting point, alter glazes with Gerstley borate, Hommel Frit 14, a lithium compound, talc or flint. Often a 5% change will give the desired effect. This is also a good way to make colorant tests. If five alterations do not give at least one satisfactory glaze, then discard the formula entirely.

**Glaze results can be varied** and controlled by manipulation of the quantity of glaze water. The technique is especially useful in oxidation firing because with this kiln atmosphere, the ceramist usually depends more heavily on application for surface variation. To demonstrate the effect, add 80, 90, 100, 110 grams of water to 100-gram dry samples. Dip test cups or tiles in the batches, and fire. The same glaze recipe may vary considerably in surface quality, depending on the amount of water in the mix.

**When making color tests** of a basic glaze, one generally uses small amounts of the glaze for this purpose—perhaps 25 or 50 grams—and after each test is painted on a test tile, the remainder is discarded. By combining two of these test amounts for an additional test, you not only can have half again as many tests, but you also may have some very striking results.

**When running triaxial blends,** label paper cups with a three-digit number representing the proportions of glaze materials A, B and C to be used for each test. For example, cup 253 would have two parts (20 grams) of material A; five parts (50 grams) of material B; and three parts (30 grams) of material C. Mark corresponding test tiles with the same three digits for easy reference.

**Onionskin typewriter paper** is ideal for placing on the scales in weighing out small amounts of chemicals. You can lift off the paper and slide the powders into the mixing vessel with no loss or muss or weight variance.

**End papers** (squares of tissue used to hold hair ends in curlers) are great for measuring small amounts of colorants for test glazes. Being so light, they require no counterbalance, and can be written on and put aside for further additions. Available at drug stores as well as beauty shops, they are inexpensive.

## Test Tiles

**Make test tiles** large and write the batch recipe for the glaze on the back of the tile with black underglaze pencil. That way, there is never any doubt about composition, and comparisons can be made quickly without referring to the glaze notebook.

**For a practical** and permanent way to identify glazes in the studio, make 2-inch test tiles and glaze these to use as identifying labels or tags for the bottles of glazes you are using. As each tile is cut from the clay slab, a hole is pierced in the corner with a sharp tool. After glaze firing, the tile is attached to the matching glaze bottle with wire strung through the hole.

**To make up glaze samples** on a board or mount test pieces on the lid of the glaze container, floral adhesive is simple to use, effective, long lasting, can be removed and is inexpensive. A small square cut off with a pair of scissors will stick your sample tile to any type of surface. When you need to change or remove it, clean off with any oil-base fluid such as salad oil, mineral oil or paint thinner.

**You can easily make** a large number of test tiles at one time by the following process. Lay four boards on a large plaster bat so that they form a frame. Pour slip onto the bat within the frame to about ¼-inch thick. Allow the slip to set up and then cut it into suitable sizes. A small hole at one end of each segment for hanging will allow you to keep a permanent record of your glaze tests.

**Do glaze testing** on handbuilt miniatures, such as flower or weed vases approximately 2 inches in height and 1½ inches in diameter (base measurement). These pots can be tucked easily into any spare spots in the kiln.

**To test a glaze,** simply dip the bottom of a cylinder in the wet batch and fire upside down. Small cylinders can be thrown off the hump, press molded or cast, and used to show how the glaze acts on both vertical and horizontal surfaces.

**Instead of making** the usual rather boring test tiles for glaze tests, throw dozens of egg cups off the hump. This is quick and easy to do, and it takes little clay. A foot can be turned and a stem shaped, if you desire. These are terrific for glaze testing because they present a variety of surfaces; they are large enough to explore all types of surface decoration, too.

**For glaze tests** make small cups (for vertical surfaces), leaving a smooth finish on the outer surface of each to facilitate writing on it with an underglaze pencil a glaze identification system which includes glaze type, source of glaze (author or book), formula or variation, colorant identification and percentage, and cone number. Glaze the interior of the cup and the upper half of the exterior, leaving the lower half free for the glaze identification. After a firing, critique the results, taking note of the color, finish, viscosity, crazing and defects.

**When making test tiles** for glaze samples, brush an often-used slip, engobe or underglaze on half of each tile and then sgraffito a few lines through the slip. Proceed as usual to bisque fire and glaze. This kind of test gives a complete picture on one tile of the effect of a particular glaze on the plain clay body, over slip and over sgraffitoed slip.

**Triaxial glaze tests** have been used for years to help the potter discover the effects of three different materials in various degrees of saturation with each other. Generally, the tiles for these tests have been made by rolling and cutting clay for this use, throwing and carving up pots or casting forms for this particular purpose. For those who might be interested in making a triaxial test tile mold for testing their glazes, choose a piece of clean, unbent chicken wire and cut from its center a triangular pattern which encompasses 21 of the little 1-inch hexagons. Then press this "die" into a slab of clay rolled out to a thickness of ¼ to ½-half-inch. Upon pulling the wire framer from the soft clay, you will discover 21 little raised islands of clay have been formed on which you may apply glaze tests.

**To keep glazes from running** together when firing triaxial blends on a flat tile, place a bottle cap on the tile and trace around it with wax resist for each proposed test. This small amount of wax should keep the glaze tests contained in a small circle on the tile.

**For a time-saving way** of making slip and glaze test tiles, throw a bowl that is fairly wide, with walls slanting out a little. Apply horizontal bands of different engobes inside and out,

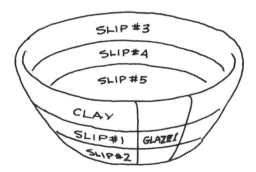

leaving one band of the original clay. Scratch the number of the engobe into the band for labeling purposes. When bisque fired, apply to the bowl vertical bands of different glazes; use one thin and one thick coat for each glaze tested. Label the glazes under the bowl.

# Glazing

## Glaze Application

**Wetting a pot** with water a few minutes before applying oxidation matt recipes can result in a glaze surface that is thinner on prominences, producing greater surface variety than normal glaze applications to a dry pot. This method sometimes achieves the subtle variety of color which is more typical of reduction firing.

**If you are working with clay** you have dug yourself, you may run into "scumming" on your bisque. This is a white surface coating from deposits of soluble salts in the clay, which is difficult to glaze. Glazing can be successfully accomplished if you brush over the scummed areas with diluted vinegar.

**To experiment** with several glazes on the same object that have close resemblance in the raw state, add a little food coloring to help distinguish between coats or glazes.

**With thinly cast or thrown pots** which must be glazed on the inside by pouring, the walls get so water soaked that it is difficult to apply glaze to the outside. Try pouring the inside one day and letting this glaze dry at least overnight. It should be much easier to apply the glaze to the outside.

**Small bisqued tiles** can be used to test glaze thickness before applying it to your ware. A typical stoneware recipe with the proper amount of water should take a three-second dip for normal coverage. Scratch through the glaze to check; the tiles can be washed and later reused.

**When spraying or brushing** a white clay body with transparent or white glaze, it is almost impossible to tell when the form is evenly covered. A few well-aimed pencil marks, drawn on the bisqueware, will give you a pattern to cover with the glaze. No tell-tale marks will be left after the firing, and no special equipment is needed.

**Potters could probably sell more** planters if the insides were completely unglazed, because most plants' roots will not grow to touch the sides of a glazed pot. Orchids are especially endangered by pots which have been glazed inside, because their roots need to adhere to the clay. If we can deliver what the plant lovers want, we can profit from it and save the wasted glaze which only the dirt will ever see.

**To handle and dry the glaze** on the bottom of a tall narrow form such as a bottle or vase without marring or otherwise damaging it, insert a narrow wooden stick of sufficient length in the neck and place the other end of the stick in an empty soft drink bottle in a carton. This serves to balance the weight and to permit all-around drying without touching the outer surface of the pot.

**Small dry sponges** aid in smoothing over little blemishes on the surface of a dried but unfired glaze. Rub the sponge over an uneven spot or a pinhole and it will scratch off the high spots and fill the holes with glaze.

**If a rubber glove** is kept with each glaze bucket, and worn when the batch is mixed or used, then switching glazes during application may be accomplished more quickly.


## Dipping

**Anyone who has dipped** a pot into a bucket of glaze knows how difficult it is to keep the form level and achieve a horizontal ring of glaze around the foot. To simplify this, purchase a small utility level about the size of a silver dollar. By keeping the two bubbles level as you dip, perfect results will be achieved every time.

**To dip hard-to-grasp bowls** for glazing, especially for purposes of side decoration, try using a loop of soft wire. Bend the wire loosely around the bisqueware in a vertical position, so that the knot is at the foot. As the form goes into the glaze in the upside-down position, the index finger is used to hold the wire taut, and the thumb and third finger prevent the bowl from tilting or slipping from the loop. If you leave a dry foot, it is quite easy to rest the bowl upside down on the other hand. When the wire is removed, the bowl can be inverted in one easy motion.

**To avoid glaze touch-ups** (fingermarks or tong blemishes) on plates or other flat ware, try this glazing technique. Apply wax resist to the bottom of the ware, attach the suction cup of a "plumber's friend" to the surface, then dip the pot evenly in and out of the glaze pail. When the glaze has dried sufficiently to be handled without damage, suction can be released and the ware returned to the shelf.

**The small, clear suction cups** often used to hold stained glass "suncatchers" on windows make good grippers for dipping objects in glaze. One holds a cup or mug quite well; use two for larger objects.

**An inverted trash can lid** is ideal for dip glazing the lips of wide bowls or other forms too large to fit in conventional glaze containers.

**A pipe cleaner** is an excellent tool for dipping beads in glaze. When this bristled wire is removed from the bead, the hole is completely cleaned.

**Golf tees** are very practical to support clay beads after glazing. Simply stand the tee on the wide end and insert the point of the tee into the hole of the bead. As soon as the glaze has dried, the beads can be moved to the firing apparatus.

## Pouring

**A standard-size garden watering can** with the sprinkler cap removed will make an excellent container from which to pour glaze. Because of its accuracy and the ease of flow control, it is especially useful when pouring glaze over large works.

**When pouring glaze,** instead of holding the pot by hand, or supporting it on a pair of sticks over a drip pan, turn it upside down on a wire coat hanger that is placed on the rim of the pan. The pan, pot and all, can be rotated while the glaze is being poured over the pot, eliminating a lot of awkward handling. The pot can be left on the coat hanger until the foot is cleaned. Because of the characteristic tapering shape of the hanger, all sizes of pots can be glazed in this convenient manner. The wire coat hanger is also a handy support for resting the sieve when glazes are being screened into a pan that is larger than the sieve.

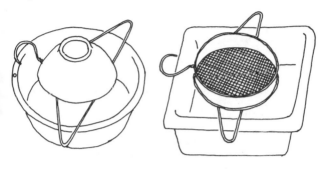

**When glazing a large bowl,** glaze the interior of the bowl in the usual manner, then invert the object and place it in the lid of a large plastic trash can. Pour the glaze over the bowl and allow it to dry before removing it. The flexible lid can easily be bent to form a spout for pouring the excess glaze back into its container. A child's swimming pool might be used in a similar manner for monumental works.

**When pouring glazes,** try using a cake rack or broiler rack—there is no splashing of glaze, the clean-up job is much easier and, best of all, you won't waste glaze that usually clings to board supports. For very large pots, an old refrigerator shelf can be used. These can be found in second-hand stores or appliance stores selling used items.

**When glazing** a bowl by pouring, glaze the interior in the usual way, but when you glaze the exterior, place a stilt inside in the wet glaze and turn the bowl upside down with the stilt resting on a support. There should be no marks at the rim from rods, and the three small stilt marks inside can be retouched with a bit of glaze.

**Thrown goblet shapes** (glazed and fired) make excellent supports when pouring glaze on the exteriors of inverted bowls. They don't mar the glaze on the interior of the ware, and there is no need to touch up blemishes on rims.

# Plugging Holes

**Push a piece of soft clay** into the drainage outlet of a planter before glazing the inside of the ware. The clay plug keeps glaze from running out, and is easily removed once glazing is completed.

**To plug the holes** in planters when applying glaze, a variety of sizes of corks may be obtained from winemaking supply shops. The corks are more convenient for this purpose than wads of soft clay, and also reusable.

**When glazing items** with holes, small pieces of kneaded eraser work well as plugs. Shape them to fit crevices, then remove them after glazing. To reuse, simply rinse off the glaze.

**Try using plastic "party picks"** to plug up the holes of salt and pepper shakers when glazing them. Simply stick the picks into the holes, dip the shaker into the glaze and pull out the picks as soon as the glaze is dry enough. Because the picks are plastic, they wash easily and the glaze can be salvaged. If the picks are too long for convenient use, they can be broken or cut in half.

**To glaze teapot strainer holes** so they will not clog during firing, sharply tap the pot on a table to jar the still-wet glaze from the holes. It is important to do this quickly or the glaze will dry in place.

**When glazing single-fired teapots,** cut strainer holes after glazing, or add a separate unglazed strainer section. Either of these methods ends losses from glaze-clogged strainer holes. When added to the fuel savings of single-firing, the cost of teapot production is greatly reduced.

# Foot Protection

**To keep glaze from running** onto the base of an object during firing, rub finely ground charcoal on the foot and base, and set the work on a kiln shelf which has been sprinkled with dry flint.

**After trimming** a pot, make a series of circular grooves just above the foot rim to help deflect a runny glaze during firing.

A **porcelain pot may fuse** slightly to the kiln shelf during glaze firing, resulting in a chipped foot. To remedy this, paint the foot prior to firing with a solution of 1 heaping teaspoon of alumina hydrate to 4 ounces of liquid wax emulsion (which has been diluted with water to the consistency of light cream). Stir the mixture frequently during application.

**Instead of using wax** to protect the bases of pots while glazing, use masking tape. It is quick, economical, may be cut to shape and equally efficient.

## Raw Glaze Removal

**A scrap piece of aluminum** and vinyl door sweep weather stripping is ideal for scraping the still-wet glaze off the flat bottom of a pot.

**A large synthetic sponge** (available in supermarkets and hardware stores) or a big block of poly foam (from a pillow or chair seat) can be used to quickly and easily clean the bottoms of ware after glazing. Saturate the sponge with water and place it on a flat surface in the glazing area. Then, after dipping each pot in glaze, set it on top of the sponge and twist in a circular motion three or four times to completely remove any residue. This method eliminates the need for scraping or further cleaning, and considerably speeds up the glazing process.

**To remove glaze** from the bottoms of ware before firing, cut a piece of nylon carpet to the size of your wheel head, stitch a straight piece of fabric around the edge, hem it, and insert elastic in the casing. Slip the carpet over your wheel head, wet this surface, and hold the bottom of each pot over the spinning wheel. To clean the carpet, pour water into the center.

**Versatile nylon net** is excellent for removing traces of glaze from bisqueware. Scrape off most of the excess with a knife, then wrap a small piece of net around one finger to finish the job. This method eliminates the need for wax resist on footrims, flanges, lips, and is effective for removing accidental drips, too.

**While decorating greenware** or bisque, beads of glaze may be removed from waxed areas by rubbing with steel wool—an easier technique than the usual wipe with a wet sponge.

# Reglazing

**Reglazing fired work** is much easier if the ware is heated in the open kiln, in the oven or under electric lamps before glaze is applied. This preheating will evaporate the water in the glaze and prevent it from running during application.

**When reglazing** a fired pot it is often difficult to make the added coat adhere to the glossy surface. To make this easier, dip a small sponge into glaze, squeeze the sponge nearly dry, and then literally scour the glaze surface with it. Used in this manner, the glaze acts as an abrasive. When the surface dries, apply the glaze coating in the usual manner. It will adhere with less difficulty.

**To aid in reglazing** pottery, mix a small amount of liquid white glue with water, just enough to paint it on the ware smoothly with a brush. When this coating is dry, apply glaze over it. The glue makes the surface rough, allowing the new coating of glaze to stick, and the glue burns out in the firing.

**To reglaze fired ware** add a tablespoon of gum tragacanth to water (about ½ cup). After about 10 minutes, work this through an ordinary strainer to remove the lumps. To this add a cup of mixed glaze. The mixture should brush on the fired pot smoothly.

**Reglazing the inside of a bowl** can be achieved quickly and easily by dipping a paper towel into glaze and placing it in the

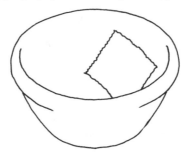

desired area. Sponge off any excess glaze that runs into the center and fire the object with the paper towel—wet or dry—in place. This procedure is recommended only for the inside of bowls and plates.

# Wax Resist

## Wax Resists and Techniques

**To make an excellent wax resist,** dial the appropriate low temperature setting on your electric skillet, and then add ½ cup of kerosene and a walnut-sized piece of paraffin. A large number of foot rims can be quickly dipped in this mixture.

**Ordinary wax crayons** can be used effectively for wax-resist decorating. The regular crayon, just as it is, can be used to draw on a bisque pot before it is glazed. The wax will resist the glaze and give an unglazed decoration after the ware is fired. You can also save scraps and pieces of crayons and melt them to make a liquid wax-resist material that can be applied with a brush.

**Try waxing feet** as you take warm ware from the kiln: Take a small candle or taper such as are used in churches and run it around the warm foot. It fits at once to the foot and will not slip. Also you can notch the candle and make the waxed area as wide as you wish. If no candle is handy, use large crayons of any color. The color burns out leaving a slight whitish residue which is rather a good finish for bare clay. If this is undesirable, it can easily be removed with a wire pan cleaner.

**Local churches can be a source** of free wax, providing a supply of candle ends which otherwise might be thrown away. When the wicks are removed, the candles can be melted in an electric frying pan.

**Add a small, scented votive candle** to your hot wax (for wax-resist decoration)—it makes your whole studio smell good.

61

**Adding food color to wax resist** makes it much easier to see where the wax is going when doing intricate brushwork designs.

**A mixture of wax resist** and sand makes an excellent separating medium for coating contact surfaces of inset lids before glaze firing. The wax retards any glaze adherence and also acts as a binder for the sand.

**Applying liquid wax resist** with the corner of a small block of foam rubber facilitates making a straight, even line, and speeds waxing. The foam usually will hold enough wax to resist a medium-sized pot before dipping again.

**When waxing the bottoms of bowls** larger than the wheel head, try doing them in pairs, rim to rim.

**Rather than wait** for liquid wax-resist designs to dry, fan them lightly with a propane torch. They'll dry in an instant.

## Wax Resist Substitutes

**One quart of wax resist** mixed with a quart of ordinary floor wax makes an excellent solution for masking foot rims and for decorative work while substantially reducing the cost.

**For a resist medium** on high-temperature ware (Cone 8 +), use waterbase acrylic (polyvinyl acetate) paint on foot rims, inside teapot flanges, or as decoration. The pots are then dipped or sprayed as usual.

This medium lends itself to use on porcelain or salt-glazed ware with the addition of equal parts alumina and flint, but mark the container to avoid confusion.

**Saddle soap** makes a good substitute for wax resist.

**Instead of coating the bases of ware** with wax resist prior to glazing, allow pots to sit for a minute or two in a pan containing about ½ inch of water. Little glaze will adhere to this saturated surface, and any residue is easily sponged away.

**For a workable glaze resist,** mix equal parts petroleum jelly and turpentine, then stir thoroughly. The mixture is easily brushed on for both fine-line details and broad areas, does not "feed" bacteria or fungi (like wax), and can be fired to at least Cone 7 oxidation with no residue.

## Wax Resist Removal

**To remove wax resist,** scrub the waxed area with a cotton swab soaked in rubbing alcohol, then clean with water.

**When wax goes** where it's not supposed to go, use lacquer thinner and it comes off easily.

**Burn away unwanted wax** with a propane torch. Too rapid heating may crack a pot because of uneven expansion, but ap-

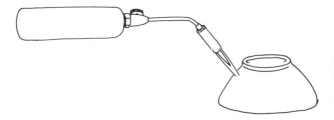

plying the heat generally and then zeroing in on the wax should prevent this. As soon as the wax blackens, it is altered to carbon, and the resisting property is lost; it is not necessary to completely burn away the carbonaceous residue.

**A helpful method** of removing unwanted spots of wax resist is to hold the offending area directly in front of a peephole for a brief moment while the kiln is operating at red heat. This is excellent for small areas and eliminates having to put up with soot or a poor job of cleaning.

**One way to cover wax-resist spots** that appear by accident on bisqueware is to scoop off some of the thicker glaze from the inside of the glaze container and dab it onto the waxed spot. The glaze should stick to the wax, preventing that empty mark after firing.

# Firing

## Stacking Ware

**When glaze-firing porcelain,** pots fire with fewer problems if they are placed on a thin layer of silica sand on the kiln shelves. But this can be a problem especially on the upper shelves—sand can very easily fall on pots underneath, ruining glaze surfaces.

A simple solution is to mix sand with wax resist and brush it on the bottom of the pots prior to glazing. When the wax dries, the particles are held firmly in place. In firing, as the wax burns off, the sand is deposited exactly where you want it with no danger to the pots underneath.

**Large bowls** of similar size and proportion may be stacked inside one another for bisque firing if each is filled with enough vermiculite to support the next bowl. Vermiculite may be repeatedly fired for the same purpose.

**For stacking** top-heavy bottle stoppers which do not fit commercial stilts or which may topple over if dry footed, make your own stilts from clay. The base of the stilt is in the shape of a Y, and there is a vertical section which fits into the hollow of the stopper. Bisque fire the stilts before using them and brush kiln wash over the whole bottom section. You should also dry foot the stopper and in this way prevent any sticking of the two parts.

**Instead of firing lids** with unglazed rims, glaze the rim, leaving the inside center unglazed. From soft firebrick (broken pieces work fine), cut small square or oblong "stilts" tall enough to raise the lid well off the kiln shelf. With white glue, attach one of these stilts to the glaze-free area on the underside of the lid and allow it to harden. This makes it easy to place the lid in the kiln, even in an awkward spot, without having to balance it on its stilt in the midst of other pots. Lids never warp using this method and the visible area of the lid receives good customer acceptance because it is glazed. The glue burns out in the Cone 8 firing and the stilts may be reused.

**When using clay pads** to level kiln shelves in stacking, roll the clay in flint, shake off the excess, and put these between stilt and shelf. After firing, the "kiln cookies" come loose easily and leave a clean shelf.

**When stacking a kiln,** put pots with flaring tops in the center of the kiln to prevent their warping during firing. These shapes need an even heat during firing, just as they need a careful drying after they are formed. Nearer the walls and elements of the kiln, place vertical pots, covered jars (with the covers fired on for bisque firing), and heavy-walled pots. These are less likely to warp and are less in need of even heat.

**To control the correct placing** of an object on a triangular stilt in a top-loading kiln, use a mirror held at a 45° angle.

**When stacking a top-loading kiln** for a glaze firing, it sometimes is difficult to place large bowls with small rims on the stilts, and to stilt the last object or two on a shelf. For these forms, glue the stilts to the foot rims with a drop of airplane-type glue at each point, then allow this to dry. In this way, you can pick up pot and stilt together and know that they will stay together. The glue burns away in the firing, of course.

**When constructing new shelves** in the studio for storing greenware or bisque, make the storage space exactly the same size as the stacking space in your kiln. With two or three such shelving modules, you will have alternatives for efficiently placing ware, and know exactly when enough pots have been accumulated for a well-packed firing.

**To identify after firing** the order in which draw rings were removed from the kiln, a system of pinch marks at the top of the rings will suffice. Set them in the kiln so that the draw ring with one pinch is at the front (the first to be removed), followed by the ring with two pinch marks, and then by one with three pinches, and so on.

**If you have warping problems** in bisque firing tiles, try standing the tiles on end in the kiln instead of placing them flat on the kiln shelves. Place them near the center of the kiln, not too close to the elements, so that the tiles receive even heat. If possible, allow a little space between the tiles for better air circulation.

A firing rack, which will enable you to place tiles vertically in the kiln, will help conserve kiln space and give better firing results. You can get better heat distribution through the kiln than if the tiles were stacked horizontally on closely spaced kiln shelves. Use an insulating firebrick and porcelain tubes to build the rack. Cut a brick lengthwise into two equal parts and insert the tubes at a slight angle. One brick can easily accommodate nine tiles.

## Firing Procedures

When trying published glaze recipes, bear in mind the firing cycles of different kilns. A glaze which works well in a large kiln, where the highest temperatures are achieved gradually, may produce unsatisfactory results in a fast-firing portable electric model, even though the specified cone has melted. Adequate time at peak temperature is necessary for complete fusion and boil out of gases in the glaze, After the cone goes down (or the shutoff trips), reset the kiln to medium for 20 minutes, then back to high for 20 minutes or so. This soaking period can help to reproduce the conditions obtained in large kilns, as indeed can slowed cooling by leaving a small kiln set at medium or low for a few hours before final shut-off.

Sulfur fumes released in bisque firing an electric kiln can be controlled by placing a small cup of whiting in the firing chamber. The same material may be used several times.

Fire pots in saggars with used teabags as a local reducing agent. Since teabags are already packaged into easily countable containers, reduction can be consistent and controllable.

You can rapidly cool the kiln without danger if you know when and how. Cooling may be rapid until the kiln is at dullest red heat or approximately 1000°F. Cooling must then be slowed down until about 500°F., after which it may become rapid again. There is considerable expansion and contraction in this temperature range, so the cooling must be slow if you are to avoid damage to the ware and to the kiln.

**Indicate kiln gas pressure** with a manometer made from a piece of clear, ¼-inch plastic tubing bent into a U-shape. This is attached to the end of the gas header and filled half full of water. Under pressure, the liquid in one leg of the tubing will lower and in the other will rise. The difference in the level is the inches of water column (WC) gas pressure. Normal house pressure is 8 water column inches, so the U in this case should be about 10 inches tall.

This simple measuring device is accurate, inexpensive and cannot get out of calibration.

**One winter day** firing to meet a deadline, the propane tanks were down to a little less than half full—normally just enough to pull off a firing. However, this day was colder than usual—in the low 20s—and as Cone 9 was starting to bend (going for a full Cone 10), the tank was getting down to about 20% and the pressure dropped to about half. The temperature was leveling out and there was no way to get more gas on such short notice. The only answer was to heat the tanks.

A quick tent was improvised around the tanks with a couple sheets of plywood and a blanket, and a truck backed up to the tent so that the exhaust blew into it. In about 5 minutes, the pressure began to rise and in another 20 minutes the firing was over.

Not an everyday procedure to be sure, but it saved the firing, and the gallon or so of gasoline burned in the truck was certainly a bargain compared to what would have been wasted had the kiln not reached temperature.

**It is possible** to have successful sawdust firings in a gas trash incinerator that vents into a masonry chimney; it is also handy when burning plant materials for ash glazes.

**At a recent workshop** for sawdust-injected firing, the sawdust had to be drawn by rotating a vacuum cleaner hose constantly. An alternate approach is an idea which operates like some bingo machines. Build a funnel or triangular-based sawdust bin in the bottom of which is mounted a rotating cylinder full of holes. Attached to this cylinder is an outside handle, which can be turned occasionally to assure movement of the sawdust. The shape of the bin does most of the work.

**As an alternative** to a large-scale sawdust kiln firing, pierce six holes approximately 1½ inches up the wall from the bottom of an empty 5-gallon paint can, and nearly fill the can with dry sawdust, packed around several small pots. Cover the top few inches with tightly crushed newspaper. Place the can into a wood stove or fireplace. Then light the paper and close the lid loosely, leaving the stove damper and air vent all the way open. When using a fireplace, the lid of the 5-gallon can should be slightly raised to allow adequate burning. The results of this firing are similar to those achieved in the larger kilns, yet this technique opens possibilities for city dwellers and others interested in less conspicuous firing methods.

**By bisque firing ware** to around Cone 2 prior to raku firing, a stronger body is formed and works don't chip or break as easily. Results can be further improved if pots are reduced in a combustible material high in oil or plant resins, e.g. eucalyptus leaves or pine needles. For those who have neither of these available, newspapers treated with a fine spray of used motor oil also work well.

**A fireplace** near the studio can give some wonderful results in light reduction of raku ware. While the glaze is maturing on a form in the kiln, prepare the fireplace floor in one of any number of ways—with crumpled paper or leaves (particularly wet ones), evergreen cuttings, rags that have been used to wax the floor or clean the car, sawdust, or sawdust sprinkled with machine oil, or wood shavings from the lumberyard. When the glaze on the pot turns shiny, take it from the kiln with raku tongs and carry it to the fireplace, allow it to reduce, then quench, if desired, in a bucket of water. There is no end to the possibilities one can get—easily, safely and without smoke in the eyes.

**For reducing raku** immediately after firing, use an old refrigerator. Break out all plastic and insulation, and, most importantly, remove the door latch for safety. Place the refrigerator back side down, and fill it with sawdust, leaves, or other reducing material.

**An insulated metal ice chest** makes a good container for reducing and carbonizing raku ware. With the lid latched securely, the smoky atmosphere is maintained, producing exceptionally lustrous, metallic glazes; and cooling is slowed when firing on a winter day.

**There seems to be timidity** on the part of some potters about doing raku in an electric kiln. Simply turn off the elements before removing your pots, then turn them on again after more ware is placed in the kiln. There is very little heat loss and no danger involved.

**When unloading a hot kiln,** grasp pots with fireplace log holders; they are also excellent for raku.

**In unloading a kiln** remove hot shelves with a 4-inch C-clamp. Slip the C-clamp under the edge of the shelf, tighten the clamp and lift the shelf from the kiln; then loosen the clamp after taking the shelf from the kiln, and repeat on the next shelf until the kiln is unloaded. Result: no burns.

## Cones and Pyrometers

**Sometimes the atmosphere** inside a firing kiln becomes rather murky and it is difficult to see the cones. In such a case, a 10-inch length of ½-inch copper tubing is an aid to checking on the progress of the cones in deforming. Place one end of the tube just outside the peep hole and blow sharply through the other end. This clears the atmosphere and allows the cones to be seen clearly and instantly through the tube.

**Use a flashlight** with a strong beam to check the progress of the pyrometric cones. The beam cuts through the atmosphere at any stage of the firing and is most efficient.

**When viewing the large cones** through a peephole try sighting through a number five tinted lens from a welder's hood. Everything can be seen clearly at the highest temperatures. You can cut a hole in a ping-pong paddle and tape the lens to it—forming a protective shield for your face.

**To reduce glare** when looking in a hot kiln, a lens can be easily made from a pair of polarized clip-on sunglasses. Cut the lenses from the metal frame and rotate one lens three-quarters of a turn so that the view is darkened but not obliterated. Tape the lenses together around the edges so that they don't shift. Hold it close to your eye and look into the kiln. Things appear as if by magic!

With this lens, cones can be set deeper into the kiln for a more accurate temperature reading; fire boxes can be viewed to the rear of the kiln at incandescent heat, and eye strain is greatly relieved.

**Trouble with the cones twisting** in the firing might be the result of the cone setter clay being of such a fine grain and shrinking so much in the drying and firing. Adding grog to the clay will open it, allowing more even drying and also reducing shrinkage.

**Eliminate the task** of making cone plaques for each firing by constructing a reusable holder. Saw a 1x1x2-inch section from the corner of an insulating firebrick, then carve slanting holes in the top surface to accommodate cones.

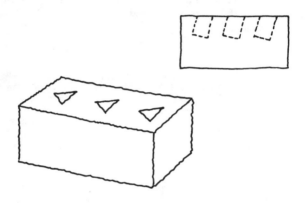

**One or two kitchen matches** inserted in the wet clay of the cone plaque provide a useful aid for checking cone placement in the kiln. Light the matches, close the kiln door, and the cones can be seen perfectly.

**Cones fired in a salt kiln** are rarely accurate because the residual salt build-up fluxes cones prior to salting, and thereafter they are obviously well-fluxed, bending too soon. But cones placed deep inside a tall vase tipped on its side will read accurately because the vase protects them from the kiln atmosphere; nor is there any noticeable temperature difference because of this protective enclosure. A vase thrown from clay with a high percentage of alumina hydrate (wedged in) will last through many firings, or standard ware may be used to enclose the cones, according to preference.

**When using low-fire cones** to indicate the time to start body reduction for a stoneware firing, the cone can be kept from melting onto the kiln shelf by mounting it in extra clay on the side of a shallow, oblong bowl 1½ inches in length and ¾ inch in width. If properly designed, the fired bowl can be used as jewelry when a hole is previously cut in one end.

**To eliminate the problem** of placing cones at the proper eye level for viewing through the peephole of a softbrick kiln, a kiln post may be attached horizontally to the wall as a shelf for cone placement. Mount a 1- or 2-inch rectangular post just below the peephole, using Nichrome or Kanthal wire looped around the post, through the soft brick, and tied in a knot against the outside of the kiln wall. A small drill will facilitate the process, especially if the kiln has a metal jacket. The supporting wire has a long life and lasts through many firings, while the cone shelf is always where it is needed, without interfering with stacking or ware placement.

**Anyone who fires very often** in an electric kiln will periodically knock the small cone from the kiln sitter during loading. To retrieve the cone, use a flexible shaft gripper, the kind used to retrieve nuts and bolts. It grasps the cone easily without damaging it. A small dental mirror can be wired to the flexible shaft to locate hidden cones.

**Taping a junior cone** to the kiln sitter when loading an electric kiln prevents the cone from being accidentally dislodged during loading of ware. The tape will burn out during firing with no ill effect on the cone or the sitter.

**A thermocouple can be protected** from the kiln atmosphere or physical damage by encasing it in a hollow, triangular shelf post (1 inch wide and 8 to 10 inches long). One end of the post is sealed with refractory mortar, then the thermocouple is inserted up to the sealed end. A triangular hole is cut into the firebrick kiln door or wall and the post/thermocouple pushed through.

**A portable pyrometer** is a good investment, especially if you have more than one kiln, because it can be made to serve any number of kilns. Merely solder an alligator clip to the end of each of the wire leads. The pyrometer then may be clipped to the thermocouple of any kiln to get its temperature reading.

Incidently, it is a good idea to have a thermocouple for each kiln. By leaving it in the kiln permanently, thermocouples will enjoy a longer life than if repeatedly stuck in and out of kilns, being subjected to rapid changes of temperature.

71

# Troubleshooting

## Defects in Ware

**Openings of wheel-thrown forms** may become distorted after being lifted from the wheel head or during the stiffening-up state. Since most objects need a circular top, these distorted ones may be put back in round. Keep an assortment of burned-out electric lamp bulbs available and revolve one of these lightly in the opening of a distorted pot to make it true again. this must be done carefully, of course, and the clay must be in the plastic stage; otherwise the action will crack the rim.

**In regard to plates cracking** during drying, the problem is more likely a matter of improper wedging of the clay or allowing creases to form during the throwing process. Very good results may be obtained with natural drying, although it may be necessary to turn large plates and bowls once or twice. Whenever you encounter cracking problems, give a little more attention to wedging, and the cracking should stop.

**When glaze crawls** away from a ceramic object in firing, leaving an unsightly bare place, rub some of the same glaze into the spot. Let this dry, then brush more glaze around the general area and refire. This should give a smooth, even glaze job with the desired results.

**Pinholing** is the presence of very tiny bubbles in a glaze, often caused by firing the kiln too fast. A fast firing does not give the normal gases a chance to escape, but traps them in the glaze in the form of minute bubbles. To correct this, the kiln should be fired in a slower cycle, with a much longer time on low and medium before turning to high.

**If sand isn't readily available** to place on kiln shelves for firing large bowls or other forms that might warp in the firing, try using a thin layer of flint. It is the same thing, only in a pulverized form. When firing shapes subject to warping, place them in the center of the shelf so they will get even heat and this will give more protection against warping.

**Warping** in the glaze firing could be due to the length of time taken to throw the ware. When a pot is begun and finished in three or four pulls, the clay does not get as soft, and there is less chance of later warping due to stresses induced by uneven moisture content.

**Inspection of a fired glaze** on a pot or test tile, by eye or with the aid of a hand lens, does not necessarily show glaze fit problems; but a thin watery slip or glaze mix smeared on the fired surface will quickly dry and reveal hidden crazing. The tiny cracks absorb a disproportionate amount of solids and reveal any discrepancies in the surface.

**If a clay body** is slightly cracked, a drop of red ink will expose the length and depth of the damage, thus indicating whether it is worthwhile to try to repair it.

**A small dab of butter** or margarine underneath a pitcher's pouring spout insures against drips.

**Put a small amount** of clear silicone sealant on the bottom, inside edge of a spout lip to make it drip-proof.

**When decorating bisqueware** with oxides, slips, etc., wear an old nylon glove on your left hand (if you are right-handed), to handle pots. This prevents getting the natural oils from your hand on the pots, and eliminates the risk of those bare spots which won't take a glaze.

**Tiny, black, pin-size dots** on overglazed ware are called peppering, and are caused by organic matter burning out of the overglaze and settling on the surface of the ware. It would be unusual for this defect to occur in a fuel-burning kiln where there is a constant draft throughout the shelves of ware, because organic matter is carried off with the flue exhaust. Thus, peppering can be eliminated by creating a draft in your electric kiln—prop the lid open slightly, and adjust your firing schedule to allow for periods when the bottom peephole plug(s) are removed. To eliminate this glaze defect, some potters leave the lid ajar so that a draft is created during the entire firing.

**To avoid cracks** and separation at junctures in wet greenware, coat the exterior surfaces with wax resist during the leather-hard stage. The wax compensates for differences in contraction rates during drying.

**Due to a change** in the composition of the natural clay body, at 2460°F pots were still porous and the glaze shivered off in sections. It was impossible to correct the body before a great many pots were produced with it, and bisque fired. To replace the feldspar and iron needed in the clay, it was necessary to experiment with various mixtures of those compounds in a very thin slip—the ware being dipped in the mixture, allowed to dry, and then coated with a normal thickness of glaze. This method saved considerable losses and might help others. The slip formula is 5 pounds feldspar to 1 pound $Fe_2O_3$ in approximately 6 gallons of water.

## Crack Repair

**A fairly successful method** for salvaging cracked greenware is to heat the object in the oven, then apply a layer of thick slip over the cracked area. Return to the oven to reheat. Again add a layer of thick slip. Repeat these two steps until the repaired area is higher than the surrounding area. When dry, sand down to match the wall. Also, when small cracks appear in a textured pot, smoothing the crack with a thin wood tool (making the crevice a little deeper) usually takes care of the crack without resorting to the usual wet application.

**A favorite formula** for mending greenware is to add a small amount of sodium silicate to some clay slip, paint this on each broken edge, then quickly press the edges together. As soon as the slip is dry, the mended area can be scraped or sanded smooth. This same material can be used to mend broken bisqueware.

**To repair cracks** or separations in ceramic objects before bisque firing, mix to a thick consistency 50% kiln cement with 50% of a slip made from the dried clay body. Use as many applications as necessary to fill the cracks. After the mixture has dried in the crack, burnish the area to remove any excess.

**To mend cracks** in bone-dry pottery, egg preserver or vinegar can be mixed with dry clay to form a thick slip. Fill cracks with the slip. It will dry very slowly and therefore should not shrink and crack again.

**To prevent cracking** and breaking of joints in ware during firing, a mixture of ⅓ gum and ⅔ water solution may be used in place of or mixed in with slip in handbuilding. When mixed with soft clay, it makes an excellent mender. It also may be used when adding handles, knobs, etc. to thrown ware.

**When a decorative addition** or knob has broken off a greenware object, rather than simply putting it back on with slip, try placing a dab of low-fire clear glaze on the break, and firing the bisque a little higher than usual. The glaze melts enough to attach the appendage more firmly in preparation for glazing and the final firing.

**Nylon flocking fibers,** mixed half-and-half with some of the clay body, may be used to repair cracks in pottery. When wet with vinegar, the plastic batch is applied either to greenware or bisque by working it into the crack. If during drying the ware cracks again, repeat the procedure until the flaw is completely covered.

**A simple mixture** that has been nearly 100 percent successful with repairing cracks in greenware and bisqueware is as follows: two parts thick slip (made of the same clay body you're repairing), one part vinegar and one part ¼-inch shredded fiber glass. This mixture can be forced into cracks or filled around chipped areas, such as lips of bowls. When dry, the area can be sanded smooth, and after glaze firing, the crack usually cannot be detected. (This formula is not quite as successful with porcelain as it is with stoneware.)

**When firing an important work,** grind some dry clay from which the pot was made and include it in the bisque kiln. If a crack develops, mix the calcined body with a solution of sodium silicate to form a thin paste. This is worked into the crack and sanded smooth when dry. If the crack was large, the object is bisqued again after mending. Then it is glazed and fired in the normal manner.

**To repair stress or hairline cracks** in bisqueware, make clay "pencils" of the same body and fire them a cone lower. For example, if ware is bisqued at Cone 05, fire the repair pencil at

Cone 06. When the pencil is drawn over a crack, dust will begin to appear from the friction; allow the particles to build up in the crack area until full. Now, complete the repair by application of glaze—the crack should not show after firing.

**To patch cracks** in bisqueware, fill them with a paste of equal parts grog and clay (passed through a 50-mesh screen), moistened with sodium silicate. Work the mixture thoroughly into cracks and allow to dry before glazing and firing.

**Try a mixture** of Alundum (a trade name for a fused alumina product) and sodium silicate for patching cracks in bisque-fired ware. When mixed half-and-half and applied in paste form, it will seal most fissures.

**For good results** in mending cracked bisqueware use a heavy nonrunny glaze. Rub the glaze well into the crack with your fingers and proceed to glaze the object as usual.

**Any chipped bisqueware** may be repaired with the following mixture:

Patching Clay (Cone 9)

| | |
|---|---|
| Ball Clay ....................................... | 20% |
| Grolleg Kaolin ................................ | 50 |
| Potash Feldspar ............................... | 30 |
| | 100% |

Mixed with water to a thick and creamy consistency, the slip is applied to the chipped area with a brush, then burnished with a finger. After drying, the ware may be glazed as usual and fired to Cone 9. The patching mixture can be "tinted" with iron to suit darker bodies.

## Lid Fit and Removal

**Before firing,** powder the rims of lids with silica flour for easy separation from the pot after glaze firing.

**Potters sometimes encounter** difficulties in the fit of a lid for a honey pot, covered jar or teapot. Perhaps a very small amount of warping has taken place, or perhaps the fit was too snug before the form was fired; at any rate, the lid may be made to fit more perfectly by grinding it against the pot. Apply oil or a paste of 100-grit carborundum to the rim of the pot and the flange of the lid, then grind these together carefully until a smooth fit has been obtained.

**When lids are fired on their pots,** try painting a solution of one-third flint, two-thirds arrowroot (a thickener available in the spice section of many grocery stores) and water on the unglazed, touching surfaces; the proportions are not critical. Stir the paint frequently during application and try to keep it off the glaze. After firing, lids should separate readily; water and a toothbrush will remove the dry flint residue.

**As strong as fired stoneware is,** there is still some "give" to it, making it easy to remove glazed-on lids by simply squeezing the rim of the pot.

**To remove a lid** which has become stuck during firing, place the lidded form in the freezer compartment of a refrigerator, allowing enough time for it to reach the freezer temperature (approximately 20 minutes). Then remove it and immediately immerse the lower portion of the form in very hot water for one or two minutes. Lift the pot from the water and strike it sharply near the lid with a wooden implement. This should separate the lid from the bottom. Repeat if necessary.

**To free inset lids** which have become fixed during firing, run an ice cube around the edge of the lid immediately after the pot is removed from the kiln. The resulting differential contraction usually frees the lid without damage; a firm pull on the lid may be required for more difficult cases. If ware is allowed to cool before the fixed lid is noticed, heat the pot in a very hot oven before giving it the ice cube treatment.

**When covered jars** are removed from the kiln after glaze firing, sometimes lids are inadvertently stuck in place, particularly where glaze recipes emit flux vapors inside the jars. A simple technique for cleanly removing the lid is to place each pot on a slowly turning potter's wheel head and expose the lid rim to two or three turns with a handheld propane torch. This slight difference in expansion should pop the lid free, without excessive stress or damage to the ware.

**An electric vibrating pencil** with a diamond point (such as those used to engrave metal) can sometimes free a stubborn lid from a pot after glaze firing by running the tip along the juncture of the lid and body.

# Fired Ware

## Finishing Fired Ware

**Ceramic-grade feldspar** is an excellent all-purpose polishing compound. Mixed with a little water and applied by hand, it should remove stubborn carbon deposits from reduced raku ware without damaging the finished glaze surface.

**Unglazed sculptural works** can be enhanced by a coat of liquid floor wax applied with a brush. It makes them easier to dust and leaves a soft sheen.

**Water-based acrylic wall paint** and water-based wood stain are effective finishes for sculpture. When dry, cover the paint or stain with a mixture of 60% glue (such as Elmer's) and 40% water, rubbing this into the surface.

**Try finishing** unfired clay sculpture with a coat of plastic resin. Works treated in such a manner appear to be glazed, have good durability with a rich, warm stoneware color. The curing of the resin is like a "chemical firing."

**When the glaze crazes** on the inside of pottery that must be waterproof, such as a flower vase, try filling the pot with milk and allowing it to stand overnight, then emptying out the milk and rinsing the vessel. This is an easier and more permanent method than that of using melted paraffin to fill the cracks.

**Silicone spray** may be applied to low-fired pottery to prevent water seeping through when pots are used for flowers.

**Rather than buying them** commercially, mirror glass disks can be cut in your own studio. Center a square mirror directly on the potter's wheel, attach with centering tool or clay, and inscribe the circumference with a felt marker as the wheel rotates. Once the circle has been marked, the glass can be cut. Hold the glass cutter firmly in both hands, resting them on a board across the splash pan. With the wheel turning slowly, press the cutter onto the glass and make a cut in one revolution. Avoid overlapping the cut, as this quickly ruins glass cutters. Remove the glass from the potter's wheel, place it on a flat surface and, with the glass cutter, make six to eight near-tangent lines from the circular cut to the edge of the glass. Gently break these glass segments away, one by one, until a circle of mirror glass remains. Practicing a few circles first on plain glass may help to build confidence and skill.

**For a more distinctive stopper** in ceramic ware, wet a piece of fresh or dried cornhusk and wrap a cork, fastening the husk ends on top of the cork with a leather thong. It will dry tight: effective as well as attractive.

**When trimming a plate** that might also be hung from the wall, use a needle tool to punch three evenly spaced holes through the foot. After firing, wire or nylon fishing line—strung through the holes—forms a triangular hanger which allows the plate to be suspended from many different positions without prior planning for decoration. Unlike a hook glued to the back, this method allows the plate to be used for both wall decoration and as functional tableware.

**Leather thongs** make attractive hangers for ceramic planters, but they rot with age and constant exposure to moisture. It is a good idea to reinforce the thongs with nylon fishline, which is not too noticeable, or to wrap brass wire around the leather to strengthen it.

**The wire bails** from 1-gallon paint cans make good overhead handles for ceramic vessels. Macramé half knots or square knots over the wire and attach it to clay loops or lugs on the ware.

**On rough foot rims** apply a thin layer of silicon sealer (found in a tube at most hardware stores) and then set the pot on a piece of wax paper until the sealer dries. After 24 hours the sealer should serve well both as a cushion and an insulator.

**A spray coating** of clear lacquer on foot rims helps to cover rough edges and grog particles which can scratch.

**Polymer or acrylic emulsion** on the foot of a pot will protect wood surfaces from scratches, and will withstand washing in the dishwasher with no adverse effects to the coating.

## Finished Ware

**Place large, bisque pots** full of water on the hot air registers to humidify your house. They look better than pans and are cheaper than commercial humidifiers. A bisque to Cone 06 is usually enough to make ware hold water without dripping, yet allowing it to rapidly evaporate through the clay walls. The pots can be decorated with slips or stains.

**Use shards** in a variety of ways to improve firing of ware. Greenware shards are excellent as a bed under forms where excessive shrinkage may cause cracking, because shards will shrink at exactly the same rate as the ware. In glaze firing, bisque shards may be used as stilting material to level shelves or posts, as protection from the flame, or to reduce the movement of volatile colorants. Bisque shards also make great fillers for cracks when sealing spaces within a bricked-up door.

**For photographing pots** an excellent backdrop is a window shade—wrinkle free, glare free, good neutral color.

**Egg cartons** make good packing material. They are clean, shock absorbent and easy to use. If two or three thicknesses are used, they provide a secure lining for a shipping box. They can be folded to fit around any object, and small works do not get lost in a mass of excelsior.

**Large department stores** are a good place to find materials for packing and shipping ware. If you ask permission, the store management is generally happy to let you remove the many plastic bags and sheets from their bulk waste bins (usually located on their loading dock).

Crumple, twist or fold the plastic according to the packing needs of each pot. For added bulk, combine plastic sheet with crumpled newspaper. Wrap delicate forms in plastic sheet, then place them in a strong container and pack popped, unbuttered popcorn around them.

**Puffed wheat** is an inexpensive, light and available answer to packing difficulties.

# Section III

# Tools

# Tools for Throwing Processes

## Calipers

**The acute angle** cut from a wire clothes hanger works very well as calipers for measuring lids for covered jars. The wire is easy to cut and bend to the exact width needed, and several hangers may be cut to different lengths to meet the various needs for measuring.

**To record the size** of the mouth of a covered jar, gently press a piece of newsprint or paper towel over the opening of the freshly thrown pot. The resulting circle is an accurate record of measurement in the event another lid is needed.

**Plastic drinking straws** that are used to cut holes in damp greenware can also be used instead of calipers to measure openings for lids simply by snipping off the length desired. They come in colors, can be numbered with marking pencils, and can be a permanent measure in the event another lid that size is needed.

**When in a pinch** for another pair of calipers, a geometric compass loaded with an extra sharp pencil works just as well.

## Cut-Off Wire

**A strand of dental floss** makes an excellent substitute wire for making a clean cut to separate pots from their bats.

**If you need** a tight cutting wire, obtain a bow saw, the type used for trimming trees, and available inexpensively at most hardware stores. Remove the blade and replace it with strong steel wire. The tension device on the saw allows extreme tightening of the wire, which makes this tool particularly useful for cutting plates from bats, and slicing slabs.

**For a cutting wire** try 4- to 15-pound test fishing line, depending on the thickness desired. It won't rust, it slips along under the pot easily, won't get tangled up and is very inexpensive.

**Guitar strings** make excellent cutting wires for severing pots from the wheel head or slicing clay at the wedging board. The heavier wires which are wound, rather than the single wire or plastic type, are best, since they do not kink and are almost impossible to break.

**A section** of discarded bicycle brake or gear cable—usually available free at cycle repair shops—makes an excellent cutting wire which resists both rust and stretching. The heavier brake cables are suitable for wedging wires, while the gear cables are more useful for cutting ware free from the wheel head. For conveniently grasped handles, clamp the ends of the cable between two nuts on a 2½-inch bolt.

**Twisted stainless steel** trolling wire makes a useful cut-off wire. Attach a flat washer to each end.

**Tennis balls,** slit and attached to a cutting wire, will prevent the wire from getting lost or reprocessed in the pug mill.

**A wooden clothespin** makes a handy cutting wire handle which may be clipped to the edge of the potter's water bucket at the wheel. Tie about 28 inches of 8-pound nylon fishing line to the spring of the clothespin and it's ready for use.

## Needle Tools

**Make a useful tool** from a heavy darning needle and an old toothbrush. Hold the needle with a pair of pliers, heat it over a flame, and stick the hot needle into the end of the plastic handle. This has many uses as a needle tool, or as a brush to apply slip, glazes and texture.

**Convert an old ball-point pen** to a heavy-duty needle tool for incising designs, piercing holes or cutting slabs. Simply remove the used cartridge of an old pen and replace it with a large sewing needle, using pliers to crimp the eye end of the needle securely into the cartridge spring. Insert the new device in the pen and you have a sturdy, conveniently grasped tool.

**An ice pick** makes a strong, hard-to-lose needle tool.

**A sharp dart** with broken feathers may be transformed into a sturdy needle tool by pulling off the feathers. A dull-pointed dart is great for signing pots.

**Pottery needle tools** sold in art stores can be bought as biology dissecting needles for much less in school supply stores.

**To avoid the wasted motion** of picking up and putting down a needle tool while throwing, try letting the fingernail on the little finger grow slightly long, and enjoy the benefits of a built-in tool.

**To make a needle tool** take a short piece of wood from the handle of an artist's paintbrush, and make a hole in the center of the widest part. Insert a threaded darning needle after putting a little glue into the hole and also on the eye of the threaded needle. To make the needle secure, wind the rest of the thread around the handle and fasten with additional glue.

**Most school metal shops** have a ready supply of partially used welding rods which can easily be ground into strong potter's needles.

**A good substitute** for a needle tool is a large stick pin inserted in a cork. It floats, too.

## Ribs

**By shaping** and gently sanding and scraping a piece of vinyl floor tile, it is possible to make a variety of ribs. They are pleasant to the touch and impervious to moisture.

**The rubber or plastic blade** of a kitchen spatula makes a great throwing rib for use on large forms such as bowls. The handle can be detached from the blade and discarded or perhaps put to some other use as a tool.

**For potters** living near coastal areas, beachcombing can produce many varied shapes of wood. Some of these have been naturally smoothed and make excellent throwing ribs.

**Thin, flexible metal ribs** can be quickly and easily cut from old-fashioned, wide-blade Venetian-blind slats with a pair of household shears.

**A flexible rib** may be cut from a flat surface of a hard plastic shampoo bottle. The rib works well for throwing or hand-building, and costs nothing.

**An expired plastic credit card** makes an excellent throwing rib or slab cutter. For additional versatility, one edge of the card can be notched to make a texturing and sgraffito tool.

**A plastic lens** from an old pair of sunglasses makes a good rib for scraping.

**Small Formica samples** make excellent substitutes for wooden ribs. These $2\frac{3}{4} \times 2\frac{1}{4}$-inch Formica chips are sometimes available free from cabinet dealers, building suppliers, or kitchen and bathroom contractors. The samples can be used as they are, or can be cut to any shape to make a versatile and durable clay-forming tool.

**Wooden rulers** make good shaping tools for throwing or handbuilding. They are the right width and thickness, and with ½-inch holes drilled in them, the surface is easily gripped even when wet.

## Sponges and Chamois

**An excellent substitute** for the oftentimes-elusive elephant ear sponge is a common plastic sponge—an oblong block usually $3 \times 5 \times \frac{1}{2}$ inches in size. The finest textured sponge (resembling a chamois) is the one to use. Cut it in half or thirds, and if possible, split it to ¼ inch in thickness.

**Used tea bags** make handy disposable "sponges" for cleaning and dampening greenware and for shaping edges. Tea bags won't spoil if they are stored after being removed from the tea cup; they can be stored moist in an extra teapot or a covered jar. They do dry out if they are left uncovered, but they can be moistened again with a few drops of water and are soon ready for use.

**An inexpensive substitute** for an elephant ear sponge is a cosmetic sponge normally used to apply makeup. These can be purchased at most variety stores in a package of three.

**Foam rubber** makes an excellent clean-up sponge. Obtain scrap upholstery foam and cut it into hand-size blocks—they are super absorbent and easily rinsed.

**A strip of chamois,** used to smooth and round the rims of ware, is sometimes hard to locate in the water bowl. Instead, use a piece of old rubber glove—its bright color is easily located, and it works just as well.

**A small strip** of thin plastic makes a good substitute for the usual strip of chamois used to finish rims when throwing.

**If you are in need** of an emergency chamois to finish the rim of a pot, try using a dollar bill. George is smooth but tough.

**An elephant ear sponge** attached with wire to the narrow end of a chopstick creates a good tool for sponging the interiors of thrown pieces.

**For removing excess water** from inside a pot that has a small opening, roll a sponge and insert it through a looped turning tool; while the wheel is rotating, touch the bottom of the pot with the sponge.

**A pinch-type clothespin** makes a good throwing sponge holder for extending your reach inside tall narrow pots. When not in use, the clothespin clips to the top of your water bucket so the sponge can be readily available.

**Attach a small fishing bobber** to the corner of your chamois to prevent it from getting lost in the throwing water.

**An extendible sponge holder** may be fabricated by wrapping a sponge around the tip of a car antenna fastened tightly with extra fine wire. Sewing the tip to the sponge will secure it from sliding.

**Instead of using a stick** with a piece of sponge tied to its end for removing moisture from the inside bottom of a tall vase or bottle, use a "nut and bolt retriever." This clever tool has spring-steel "fingers" at one end that tightly clasp the sponge. One of these tools can be purchased at an auto supply store for a very low price.

It is also useful for removing scraps of trimming clay from the bottoms of tall forms with narrow necks.

## Trimming Tools

**Some excellent material** for making pottery tools can be found lying along the curbs of city streets. Thin strips of spring steel, about ⅛-inch wide and from 6 to 10 inches long, become detached from the brooms of street sweeping machines, and can be easily formed into footing and cutting tools of various shapes.

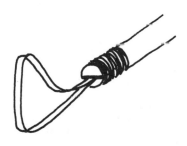

**Strap metal** from packing crates will make an excellent trimming tool. Bend a 12-inch length in half to form a loop tool; wrap tape around the ends to form a satisfactory handle. Angled shapes may also be achieved by crimping the loop.

**A Stanley Surform Shaver,** available in most hardware stores, makes an excellent trimming tool. This small wood-working device has numerous little toothlike blades, which completely eliminate chattering. It trims efficiently, easily and without much pressure (no more sagging plates), and leaves a decorative pattern which may be removed with one pass of an ordinary trimming too.

**Bobby pins** make excellent emergency loop tools which can be used as is, bent by hand, or if you are really fussy, bent in a variety of shapes with a a pair of needle-nose pliers. If you find the bobby pin too dull for trimming, sharpening with a broken piece of kiln shelf will put on a nice edge. After using such readily available materials at zero cost, some potters begin to forget the emergency aspects, and wire a bobby pin to a stout handle for a permanent loop tool.

**Cut the end(s)** off an empty ball-point cartridge, then cut a narrow strip of very thin scrap metal, approximately 3 inches in length. Bend the strip of metal into a square or round shape, insert the two ends into the cartridge, squeeze in a little epoxy glue, and allow it to harden. The resultant loop and handle make an excellent small trimming tool.

**Instead of a conventional** trimming tool, use a fine wire for trimming wheel-thrown pots such as planters. Just hold the wire tautly at the desired angle, and as the wheel turns, a shape can be quickly refined or excess clay removed. If the work is heavily grogged, the thumb can be used for the final smoothing.

**A bent tablespoon** or teaspoon when sharpened on the bowl edges makes an excellent footing tool.

**Make a trimming tool** for heavily grogged pots from a coat hanger. Straighten the hanger and bend it, bringing the two ends together. Tape the ends together with freezer tape. The closed end (trimming end) can be squared or rounded. Then use a grinding wheel to flatten and sharpen it. It lasts forever, and costs nothing.

**Before finishing foot rims** with a conventional trimming tool, use a 4-inch section of coarse hacksaw blade to trim uneven bottoms of bowls or plates. The serrated edge does not catch on rough edges, and it quickly prepares surfaces for finishing touches.

**When one of your** Japanese brushes wears out, save the handle and cut each end to serve a specific need. A bamboo tool cut to a sharp point is especially useful for many purposes, including sgraffito decorating and trimming excess clay from the bottom of a thrown pot just before it is removed from the wheel. The ends of bamboo can be shaped quite simply on an electric grindstone or other device, and can be sharpened easily if they become dull through use.

# Tools for
# Hand Processes

## Handbuilding Tools

**Bean bags** make good weights for holding work steady at any angle.

**Much time can be saved** when doing coil and slab work by employing a discarded toothbrush. Just dip the brush in water, then use it to roughen the edges that are to be joined. This method provides both scoring and "built-in" slip.

**A dog "slicker" brush** is an excellent tool for quickly scoring large slabs and clay additions. Run the brush along the table edge to remove clay buildup when dry.

**Talcum powder containers** can be filled with ball clay, grog, etc., for easy sprinkling.

**In order to redampen pots** for any kind of surface work, use an old cleaning liquid atomizer filled with water. It distributes the water evenly, is always handy and stores easily.

**An inexpensive plant mister** sold in garden centers and most hardware stores makes an excellent tool for dampening pots, slabs or slab constructions that have begun to get too hard. The fine water mist evenly wets the clay surface without excess running or dripping that could disturb fine textures or surfaces.

**Dip a wooden dowel** in shellac and when the shellac is very sticky but not dry, wind on a thin layer of fine steel wool and let dry. This makes a very useful tool for cleaning up around handles and other hard-to-get-to places on greenware.

**A section of nylon hose,** when filled with sand, makes an excellent tool for paddling extremely curved surfaces.

**A plastic shampoo bottle** filled with sand and slipped into a sock makes a good paddle for thrown or handbuilt ware. For variety, burlap or cord may be epoxied on the surface.

## Cutting tools

**When making honey pots,** use a flexible metal rib for the excised area on the lid. By bending the rib in an arc and slicing down through the leather-hard clay, you can get a perfect horseshoe-shaped notch.

**A pizza cutter** may be used in conjunction with a straight edge or ruler to produce clean lines when cutting slabs.

**The handiest gadget** for cutting slabs of clay is the roller cutter used by paper hangers. This is particularly useful when you work with drape molds.

**A pastry cutter** with blunt stainless steel blades is an ideal tool for cutting off large or small chunks of clay from the supply bin. It is especially helpful for preparing easy-to-handle blocks when unloading a barrel of plastic clay.

**Linoleum cutting tools** are excellent for incising, texture, cutting and inlay. These usually come in sets, including a holder and several different cutting heads, scoops for rounded or V-shaped cut-outs of various widths, and a blade for trimming. The V-scoop is particularly handy for making grooves in the reverse sides of slabs for tiles, greatly retarding warpage.

**An old hacksaw blade** with one end cut to a point makes a great fettling knife for leveling and trimming pots. The hole in the other end allows the blade to be hung easily from a hook or nail.

**Discarded hacksaw blades** may be bent to form clay "rakes" for applying texture to clay surfaces, or they may be cut into short lengths, then shaped and sharpened to form shop knives. Both the rakes and knifes can be easily mounted in broomstick handles which are slotted to accommodate the ends of the blades, and then bound with wire.

**To cut insulating firebrick** use an old hacksaw blade with a serrated edge, made by touching the blade (still in the saw frame) to the corner of a grinding wheel at ¼- to ⅜-inch intervals. This rough edge is excellent for cutting bricks. When the blade dulls, put it to the grinding wheel again.

**A scalpel** from a dissection kit is great tool for cutting slabs. It leaves a sharp, clean cut without tearing the clay as a needle tool often does.

**A swivel-bladed vegetable parer** is a good tool for peeling or trimming slices off leather-hard pots. After some practice, you can trim any rough spots or bumps with speed.

**Aluminum containers** that certain brands of cigars are packaged in make excellent cutting tools. After cutting off its closed end, the tube may be formed into various shapes that can then be used to cut out clay when it is leather-hard.

**Instead of discarding** a fettling knife that has lost its temper, bend the tip. The resultant tool is extremely useful for cleaning up the edges of handbuilt and thrown constructions in difficult-to-get-at curved areas without gouging.

**The working parts of a pipe wrench** make an excellent, inexpensive tap and die set for making screw-top ceramic containers.


# Tools for Drilling Holes

**The spokes of a large umbrella** can be cut into manageable lengths and sharpened to make good piercing tools for strainer holes in teapots.

**A fine-quality and inexpensive tool** for cutting teapot strainer holes may be made by inverting a lettering pen point in its pen stave (handle). The C-shaped end of the pen point will cut the clay wall cleanly with a twist and, when removed, will excise the clay plug.

**Use steel drill bits** for piercing holes in leather-hard or bone-dry clay. These bits come in a variety of sizes, and their keen cutting action will not damage fragile ware.

**A toothpaste tube cap,** glued over the end of a piece of wood dowel, makes an excellent device for piercing tapered holes in ware. The small grooves on the surface of the cap make secure grips for small candles or stoppers.

**Large soda straws** can serve as excellent piercing tools for strainer holes in teapots.

**Holes can be cut** in leather-hard clay with an expended brass shell from a rifle or shotgun. If you have access to military-type shells, M-16 brass forms small holes for leather straps, while .30- or .45-caliber shells produce larger holes for rope or drainage on planters. The metal part of a 16- or 20-gauge shotgun shell will cut larger holes. Cut or file off the primer end of the spent shell so the cuttings can pass through.

**The cap from a spent felt-tip pen** is excellent for making clean-cut drainage holes in planters.

**Many potters hang their glaze test tiles** on hooks or wire them to the glaze bottles for easy reference. Punching holes in the clay when making these tiles can be a problem, however, and here is a neat and easy method of doing this task. Place the damp cut tile on a slab of damp clay, then push the flat end of a small dowel rod through the tile. The clay slab below receives the displaced clay plug from the tile, giving a clean, trim hole. This same technique can be used to punch holes for any slab project.

**When making holes** for salt and pepper shakers, insert broken pieces of thin spaghetti into the clay before it becomes leather-hard. The spaghetti will burn out in the bisque firing, leaving smooth, rounded holes.

## Extruders

**A simple, inexpensive** clay extruder can be made from a hand-operated caulking gun, an 8-inch length of 1½-inch-diameter white PVC water pipe, a 2-inch-diameter large-holed (1¹³⁄₁₆-inch) washer, and a selection of dies.

The large washer fits inside the caulking gun and butts against the end of the PVC pipe. As the caulking gun ram is a close fit, the PVC pipe should be beveled inside at the back end. (This is simply done by angled scraping with a knife.)

For dies, use ⅛-inch-thick aluminum and ¹⁄₁₆-inch-thick steel disks drilled with a hole from ⁵⁄₁₆- to ½-inch-diameter for coil extrusion; a supplementary half-disk to produce coils with a flat side; and a die for ribbon extrusion.

Clay is hand rolled into an 8-inch plug about 1½ inches in diameter. This is gently slid into the pipe (if the clay is soft, a coating of dry clay prevents sticking), which is then placed in

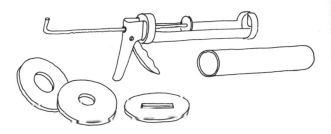

the gun. The large washer and the desired die are inserted at the front end of the pipe, and the ram is pressed forward against the clay. The ramrod is then oriented to engage the trigger; coils 8 feet or longer are readily formed. Half coils should be placed with the flat edge on the table to keep them from curling.

**When extruding** very soft forms through fired clay dies, it is a little awkward to pull the handle, support the form and cut it evenly. Try constructing an oversize cheese cutter of wood and wire by cutting out a rounded Y-shape with a hand jigsaw and adding an extra cross board to increase tension on the wire. The wire should be just long enough to drag across the bottom of the extruder for an even cut.

**It is difficult to extrude** small shapes from a pugmill because of the great force exerted as the clay presses on the unpierced part of the die. To overcome this, cut the die with the desired shape and an adjoining "waste" shape. A wire may be installed between these shapes so the desired portion will be cut, then fall away or can be lifted from the rest of the pug.

93

This principle applies to any shape with a straight cut along one side, and has proved a simple but effective means of making handles, rims and other parts for addition to studio production.

**For a quickly made** extruder die, trim a disk from a plastic detergent bottle with a razor blade to the diameter of a clay extruder. Cut a design opening, and place the plastic on a metal or bisqued-clay die—close in diameter, but not exceeding the new extrusion design. When used in the extruder, the original die will support the plastic and hold it in place.

**An inexpensive cake decorator** can be used to extrude clay shapes for addition to ware. Fill the tube with a smooth clay mixed to the consistency of stiff frosting, then extrude the contents onto a newspaper or bat to eliminate air bubbles and water pockets. Reload the decorator with the "pugged" clay and proceed to form the desired shapes. If there is more clay than needed at one time, simply wrap the tube in plastic and store for future use.

**If you have a pug mill** and an extruder, cut a pug mill die about ½-inch smaller in diameter than your extruder barrel, and produce solid pugs, slicing each to the maximum useful length of the extruder. Large quantities of the pugs can be wrapped in plastic and stored in an old refrigerator ready for immediate use without the hassle of handforming clay to fit the extruder barrel.

## Modeling Tools

**Find driftwood** on the beach and convert it into modeling tools for making pots. The wood is especially hard, smooth and holds sharp edges well. It allows the forming, at no expense, of any tool needed, either by picking up a suitable shape or by sanding it to fit specifications.

**To manufacture** your own stick modeling tools, cut a ¼-inch or larger dowel into 6-inch pieces. Using a grinding wheel or rough sandpaper, grind one end to a sharp point, the other to a wedge shape.

**Recondition** the worn, chipped or broken ends of wooden clay modeling tools by reshaping them on a grinding wheel.

# Rolling Pins

**One of the handiest tools** is a plaster rolling pin made by filling a cardboard paper-towel tube with plaster. Close up one end of the tube, pour in the plaster and, when it is set, strip off the cardboard. Cardboard remaining on the plaster may be washed off; ridges from the tube remaining may be trimmed away with a knife. The best feature of this homemade tool is that it can be dampened before use and it won't stick to the clay that is being rolled.

**A length of steel pipe** is ideal for rolling out large slabs. Sometimes called "iron" pipe, it is available at any plumbing supply store, comes in varying diameters, and can be cut to any length. It does not warp or bend, and its extra weight allows one to exert more force on the clay, thus reducing the time needed to roll out large slabs.

**When doing large slab work,** a large wooden dowel (approximately 1¼ inches in diameter) is a good and inexpensive substitute for the traditional rolling pin.

**The wooden or cardboard roller** from a window shade makes a good wide rolling pin for slab work.

**A length of sewer pipe** (5-inch diameter) works well for rolling out clay slabs. The size and weight make it easier to use than a conventional rolling pin, and discarded tiles are often available free at construction sites.

**Roll slabs** with a piece of rock drill core picked up from an old mining site; it is far superior to a wooden rolling pin. It is strong, a good weight, and it doesn't stick to the clay.

**An old roller** from a wringer-style washer makes an excellent and inexpensive rolling pin. The roller is heavy enough for easy rolling, and wooden handles can be made and attached to the shaft on each end, if desired.

**If you have trouble** finding a rolling pin long enough to roll out really large slabs of clay, you can use a discarded extra-long legal-size typewriter platen. These may be begged or bought from a typewriter repair shop.

# Decorating Tools

## Brushes

**Because paint brushes** made of foam rubber wash out easily, they are ideal for applying wax resist. They are also handy for removing excess water from the bottom of a deep pot.

**Keep a set of brushes** for use with light colors and another set for dark colors to avoid contamination of glazes. Mark the ends of the brushes for light and dark, and keep them in separate containers. You might also keep a set of special brushes just for use with clear glaze.

**One of the most useful brushes** for applying large areas of glaze as well as for obtaining some stunning large brush stroke effects in decorating, is a discarded shaving brush. It is particularly fine for the majolica technique of decorating on top of an unfired white glaze with a stain or colored glazes.

**Old eyeliner and mascara brushes** are handy decorating and cleanup tools. The eyeliner brushes are particularly useful for painting small, thin lines on greenware or bisque, while the mascara brushes are good scoring/texturing devices or aids for removing glaze from teapot strainers and planter holes.

**Good brushes for decorating** are not an extravagance if the brushes are given good care. Brushes should be thoroughly cleaned after each use in order to avoid color caking at the base of the ferrule. They should be stored in a vertical container, hair up; for a long storage period, brushes should be put in a closed container along with some moth balls. Finally, never use brushes with oil colors unless they are used only for oil colors.

**If you find it difficult** to put a smooth, rounded edge on small objects, cut down the bristles of a worn decorating brush to about ¼ inch from the metal ferrule. Dip the brush in water, dab out excess moisture on a cloth or sponge and run the damp, fairly stiff bristles around the edges of the forms. It smooths them up easily and quickly.

**An aid to cleaning brushes** when glazing ware is to put a piece of wire mesh in a plastic pail so that it rests about 2 inches from the bottom of the pail. The sediment drops to the bottom and the water remains relatively clear.

**To clean wax-resist brushes,** put rubbing alcohol into a wide-mouthed, lidded container. Simply swish the bristles back and forth a few times and pat dry. Brushes which are heavily caked can be cleaned by soaking for a period of time.

The removed wax will settle to the bottom of the container, so periodically, you can decant the clear alcohol, clean out the container, refill and you're back in business.

## Glazing Tools

**For glazing control,** try applying glaze with a turkey baster. In addition to convenience, the device offers several possibilities for decorative work.

**A paint roller** makes a useful tool for slip or glaze application. Use the shaggy kind designed for concrete block painting to hold relatively thick glaze—the surface will be smooth and even. Use standard rollers for slip where less coverage is needed. Paint rollers come in many sizes which offer a variety of decorative possibilities.

**A "long-finger,"** the kind used for removing pickles or olives from tall jars, is very useful in dip glazing very small objects. It also is very convenient for holding them when brushing on glaze. The fingers may be found in the housewares section of department stores.

**Cotton swabs** make cheap, disposable (and often reusable) luster applicators. They are good for covering large areas and do not streak like brushes often do. If you give the wad of cotton an extra twist it stays on the swab longer.

**Keep a box** of small pieces of sponge of different textures and shapes for decorating. In order to get the true texture of the various sponges and to conserve underglaze colors as well as overglazes, brush the color onto the sponge rather than dip it into the color. For this reason each impression is similar (instead of the first being solid imprints from clogged holes), and several can be made with one brushing.

**A tjanting,** or wax-writing pen used for batik, makes an excellent tool for applying liquid wax when drawing a resist design on clay. It allows more control, can produce a thinner line than a brush, and is especially useful for detailed work.

**Discarded hypodermic syringes,** such as the throw-away kind used by doctors and nurses, are excellent for exact measurement of small amounts of liquids. Use them for adding water or gum to glazes and for mixing small quantities of underglazes to obtain lighter or darker colors.

## Rolled Decoration

**To make texturing roulettes,** cast a ¾-inch-thick plaster slab in a shallow container. When it is bone dry, cut it into disks with a 2-inch-diameter hole saw, then carve textured designs in the cut edge.

**A wooden clothespin** makes a good handle for a roulette impression tool. Simply mount a wood, metal, or plastic disk between the tines with a small nail. This holds the decorating wheel in place, and acts as an axle on which the wheel rotates for infinite bands of pattern.

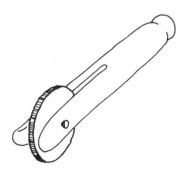

**Relief designs** cut in old rubber printmaking brayers make nice textures and patterns on leather-hard clay slabs.

**Incise woodcut designs** into a rolling pin for efficiently produced patterned slabs. Several rolling pins with varying designs may contribute to a single composition.

## Sgraffito

**Try using a tile cutter** for sgraffito. Small and easily manipulated, its tungsten carbide tip never seems to wear down.

**When scratching designs** through slip, a small hand-held rubber ear syringe (available at drugstores) is helpful in eliminating carving dust from the crevices. The syringe may be pointed in any direction and the quick puff of air will not damage work.

**Pins, pencils,** old ball-point pens and nails all work well for drawing on leather-hard pots, but an electric engraver such as a Dremel model 290 really gives a nice line.

**The life** of thin steel-loop tools used for incising and sgraffito can be increased significantly by applying a blob of Super Glue to the base of the wire.

**When scratching a design** through glaze for a decoration, a well sharpened ordinary pencil gives a better result than nibs or sharp tools, which tend to chip into the glaze and give a ragged effect instead of a clean linear one. Although the process is a bit slower with a pencil point, the resulting even and sharp edge is well worth the extra time. All pencil marks disappear in the firing, of course.

## Slip Trailers

**Local beauty salons** can be a source for obtaining plastic tube-top bottles suitable for slip trailing. Used to apply permanent wave solution, these disposable containers can leave thin slip lines from ¹⁄₁₆ to ⅛ inch in width.

**For potters** who wear contact lenses—a wetting solution bottle makes an accurate applicator for trailing fine lines of slip.

**An ordinary bulb ear syringe** is a handy tool to use for filling in ceramic inlay decorations. For best bonding action, trail the slip onto the form when the clay is at the leather-hard stage, and be sure that the slip is made from the same clay as is the ware. If you don't have an ear syringe at hand, a plastic squeeze bottle dispenser also works very well for this purpose.

## Stamps

**Potters whose studios** are sufficiently established to remain in one location may benefit from impressing damp ware on the foot with a readily available rubber address stamp. Intended for adding a name, return address and zip code to mailed envelopes, the stamp is a constant reminder to a customer, a billboard to visitors, and a direct retail link for those who bought elsewhere through a wholesale outlet. As more work is produced, so the quantity of this free advertisement also increases—constantly building sales. Stamping the potter's name and city is traditional to Early American salt-glazed pottery, linking this practice to our own heritage.

**Rather than sign** your pots, use a stamp of clay: Take a piece of fine-grained clay, roll it out to ½ inch thickness, allow it to become leather-hard, then, with a pointed tool, engrave your "mark" being careful not to chip the clay when working. Next, take a piece of soft clay and press it into the mold (with the name or mark incised) using pressure; then cut the clay (square around the design) leaving a border on the pressed clay. At this stage, take a piece of clay the right size to fit the back of the stamp to use for a handle and press it on securely, then carefully pull the clay stamp off the mold and let it dry. After drying and firing, it is ready to use.

**Small rubber stamps** from a child's printing set are available in many toy stores; even the smallest size imprints legibly on clay. To keep from losing the letters, glue them to the ends of small sections of dowel. They can be stored in alphabetical order by drilling appropriate-sized holes halfway into a scrap of $2 \times 4$ lumber.

**Wine corks** with plastic heads—such as those found on Almaden or Inglenook bottles—make excellent tools for stamping patterns into clay surfaces. The pattern may be cut with a razor blade or burned in place, and the corks are appropriately absorbent, so they pull away cleanly from the ware.

100

**Soapstone** (or other soft stone) is an excellent medium for carving a potter's mark or an impressing stamp. The stone can be obtained from hobby or craft shops, hacksawed into workable sizes, then carved with an X-acto knife. In use, the nonabsorbent surface of the stone makes clear impressions in moist clay.

**One method** for imprinting clay with letters is alphabet noodles, the kind used for making soup. They can be used on soft clay very easily for printing names, dates or anything one wants to say. If they are pressed into the clay until they are even with the surface, they can be left in through the first firing. They will burn away, leaving a perfect impression. The depressions can be accentuated with stain, colored slip, or a contrasting color of glaze.

**For those who want to stamp** lettering into moist clay, deeply carve the words or letters desired into a smooth plaster bat with a needle tool. Press a wad of clay firmly against the carving, and then form a handle on the wad. Bisque the piece and use it as a stamp. Lettering can be of any size and need not be in a straight line; the original carving can be saved for replacement stamps if needed.

**Two-part porcelain insulators** which were used to fasten wires by the old method have intricately patterned adjoining surfaces which make great stamps for impressed decoration.

**Some very simple tools** can be made from small amounts of plaster left over from a casting project. Make small mounds of the plaster, let them stiffen, then carve designs into the flat surfaces while the plaster is still easy to incise, and before it hardens completely. All sorts of designs, patterns and textures can be made easily, particularly those that might be used for repeats on a slab of clay.

**Carved linoleum blocks** used in printmaking make excellent, durable stamps for leather-hard clay.

**File flat-headed nails** of various sizes into different shapes for stamped impressions.

**The seashore** affords the alert beachcomber a multitudinous bounty of design makers in the guise of shells, sponges, coral, seed pods and weathered bits of wood.

**When you require** intricate, impressed decoration from metal, wood or plastic stamps, coat these with spray vegetable oil and they will easily release, with no clay stuck in the stamps' fine detail.

**Sprinkle talc** liberally on clay to prevent stamps getting stuck after repeated use. Talc can also help prevent clay from sticking to rolling pins and working surfaces. Baby powder is ideal.

**A plastic dry-cleaning bag** may be placed on top of a clay object prior to impressing with a bisque stamp to produce a smooth-edged decoration and prevent clay buildup on the stamp. With the plastic, even nonporous objects such as tin cans, bottle tops, cake cutters and forks can be impressed; deeply textured surfaces provide the best decoration.

**When using a bisque-fired stamp** or any object to imprint moist ware, a buildup of clay may occur causing a loss of stamped detail. Laying a single layer of a 2-ply Kleenex tissue over the clay will form a protective film between the stamp and the ware and yet not impair the quality of imprint.

## Stencils

**To mask bisqueware** for glaze designs, draw the desired pattern on contact paper. Cut out the drawn shapes, remove the backing and press the contact paper on the dry bisque-ware, rubbing from the center of the design toward the edge. Press firmly along the edges of the pattern to form a seal between paper and clay body. (Warmth from the hand should make the contact paper more flexible and allow it to conform to irregularities on the surface.) Dip the ware in glaze as usual, allow it to dry slightly and remove the contact paper with tweezers or a needle tool. When completely dry, the unglazed portion of the pot may be filled with another recipe using a syringe or brush.

**Try putting paper patterns** onto wet clay objects, then paint or dip the ware into a slip of contrasting color. When the paper is removed, the color of the clay body will be exposed. Variations of color can be achieved by adding more paper patterns and repainting or redipping the forms into a different color.

**Exposed X-ray film** is most effective for making stencils to be used for decorating or masking. It is flexible enough to go around curved surfaces; wetting will not damage it; it can be used over and over again; and its transparency often helps if a design calls for laying one stencil on top of another.

The film is best used if it is first cleaned of the dark emulsion. This comes off easily if the film is soaked in hot water for about an hour.

**For stencil decorating,** Scotch tape instead of wax resist works successfully on bisque or dry greenware. The tape can be cut out into many different shapes and applied with ease, providing the curves in the object are not too steep. Once the glaze has been applied, merely peel off the tape stencil.

## Texture Makers

**For a very effective** texture tool, remove the cutting edge from a box of aluminum foil or wax paper. The fine-toothed edge of the metal produces uniform scratch lines.

**A versatile texture tool** may be made by "fringing" the edge of a strip of copper window screen. Unweave it until the fringe is about ½ inch long. Roll the screen as tightly as possible, wrapping the "handle" part with adhesive tape for comfort. The fringe will be like a stubby brush and can be used on dry, leather-hard or moist clay.

**A metal florist's "frog"** (used for arranging flowers) makes an excellent tool for decorative scoring of clay surfaces, as well as roughening areas to be joined.

**A grapefruit knife** is ideal for texturing leather-hard clay.

**For stringlike** strand decoration, press a lump of plastic clay through an ordinary kitchen garlic or lemon press; these are available at grocery stores or gourmet shops and are fairly inexpensive.

**A kitchen grater** (the large hole variety) is a functional device for making decorative clay shapes to be applied on ware. Repeated patterns are especially easy to produce since the grater cuts many similar shapes with each use.

# Mixing Tools

## Mixers

**There is an excellent tool** in the kitchen for preparing glazes or slips—the blender. When preparing your batch of slips, you can use moist clay, leather-hard clay or even clay that is dry. For small test glaze recipes, the blender will work almost as well as the mortar and pestle.

**A portable electric kitchen mixer** is an excellent tool for mixing glazes.

**An electric bass fishing motor** makes a serviceable blunger. It is waterproof and many have three speeds in forward and reverse. By tightening it securely to the side of a galvanized garbage can, it will mix large batches of glaze or slip.

**Stirring well-settled glazes** can be a real chore, but a rotary wire paint stripper added to a 1- or 2-foot extension bit on a variable-speed electric drill will provide ease of stirring. Because the stripper is flat on the bottom and the wires are flexible, it stirs up all the glaze from the bottom and corners of the bucket. To clean the stripper between stirring various colors, just spin the excess off, then spin it clean in clear water.

**A flexible but strong** glaze mixer may be fabricated from the rubber disk that comes with a power drill sanding attachment. Drill eight ½-inch-diameter holes through the disk and remove the metal arbor (usually held in place by a screw). Weld a 14-inch length of ¼-inch-thick steel shaft to the arbor and reassemble the mixer. The rubber blade should mix thick slips and glazes easily, yet reach into the bottom configuration of any bucket; also, it won't chew up plastic buckets like metal blades do.

**An excellent stirring tool** for glazes which have settled is a sturdy bathroom bowl brush. The loop shape encourages rapid mixing, and the bristles easily dislodge caked and settled glaze from the bottom and sides of the bucket; the brush is designed to rinse clean.

**A canoe paddle** is excellent for stirring thick clay or glaze slurry in large containers.

**When glaze has thickened** in the bottom of the jar, use a sturdy, wire-loop clay sculpture tool. It cuts into the thickened glaze and in a very short time you have it in suspension.

**For mixing glazes** by the gallon (or lesser amounts) without sifting or screening, purchase a wire beater from a hardware store. It has a stiff wire handle with a wire loop at the end which is wrapped round and round with thinner wire resembling a spring coil (total length is 12 inches). This type beater takes out every lump and mixes the whole batch to creamy perfection in about 30 seconds . . . a miracle worker.

## Sieves and Strainers

**To fabricate** a great, economical screen that will not rust, purchase a 12-inch length of brass screening in the desired mesh at a hardware store. Obtain from a paint or pastry store a 4- or 5-gallon plastic bucket with a lid that does not exceed 11 inches in diameter. Cut about 4–5 inches off the top of the

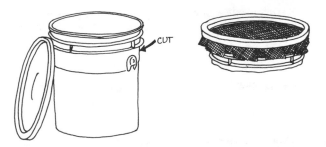

bucket, then cut away the inside of the lid, leaving only the outer lip band. Laying the screen over the top part of the bucket, snap the lid band over the screen and onto the bucket rim. This should stretch the screen tight, ready for use.

**Why pay high prices** for plastic or metal framed screens? Instead, throw a simple bowl, trim a foot ring, then excise the bottom, ¼ inch from the foot. Cut two holes in the rim to facilitate hanging with a leather strap. After firing, cut a circle from brass screening of the desired mesh, and epoxy it to the bottom of the bowl just inside the foot.

In addition to the advantage of price, these screens can be made any size to exactly fit your glaze containers.

**When you have** only a small test batch of glaze to prepare, use a regular mesh sieve modified in the following way: Use masking tape to cover the screen, except for a 2-inch square. Overlap the edges of the tape for a good seal. This small area will direct the glaze into the small-mouth jars many people use for containing test glazes. Just make sure the sieve is dry when applying the tape, and it will stay in place and withstand several washings.

**A large milk strainer** of the type used in dairies will make an excellent sieve. It is big enough for large batches of glaze and has a very fine mesh. You can find one at most hardware or farmers' co-op stores.

**An excellent sieve** for a 5-gallon batch of glaze is a "painter's sock," sold through shops where painters' tools are carried. It fits into a 5-gallon bucket, wraps around the outside and allows one to mix the harder-to-dissolve elements into the glaze by pulling the sock out and "milking" it. The nylon mesh is medium fine.

**Stirring glazes** with a kitchen strainer finds and eliminates lumps and debris fast. The lumps are pushed through the mesh while the debris is caught. Strainers with horns (for resting on bowls) are especially good for getting solids out of the bucket corners.

**A ¼-inch-mesh screen** placed over the scrap bucket helps prevent the loss of tools or sponges accidentally left in the throwing water.

**A coarse, household strainer** is a great help in separating the pebbles from the glaze after ball milling. The larger and coarser the strainer the better. For a dry glaze, shake the pebbles vigorously in the strainer. This will usually clean them quickly and easily. For a wet mix, use a small amount of water over the pebbles after shaking thoroughly.

# Section IV

# The Studio

# Equipment

## Ball Mills

**Some glaze ingredients,** when wet, do not always mix well, which results in small bumps in the glaze surface which persist after firing, especially in matt glazes. A simple ball mill can remedy this: Form ¼- to 1-inch-diameter porcelain balls and fire them to maturity. A plastic jar serves well as the mill and should be chosen according to the size of the batch—the weight of the balls in the mill should be equivalent to the weight of the dry ingredients. Five minutes of shaking by hand with a rolling action results in a smooth and creamy glaze.

**A lidded, plastic gallon jar** with five or six 1-inch steel ball bearings inside can serve as an inexpensive dry mixer. The container is filled with glaze ingredients, the lid taped in place, and the jar rolled back and forth with sufficient speed that the ball bearings tumble freely. A thoroughly mixed batch results, and the steel bearings have no noticeable effect on the fired glaze.

**An inexpensive substitute** for a ball mill is a small rock tumbler. Handmade porcelain balls for grinding should provide excellent results. It does take a little longer time to mix a batch of glaze than it would in a conventional ball mill, because the rock-tumbler barrel is rubber lined. It is best not to use a tumbler with a metal barrel, because rust from the barrel will contaminate the glaze.

**Two used typewriter rollers** (which you can easily find, usually free) make excellent rollers for a ball mill. They can be easily adapted because they have their own bearings and usually the proper size shaft for a standard pulley wheel.

# Damp Boxes

**Convert old discarded refrigerators** into damp boxes and storage cabinets. All that is necessary to convert the refrigerator to your own use is to remove the cooling mechanism. It also is important to insure the safety of children who might have access to the box by taking off the catch. Masking tape can be used to hold the door safely closed.

If the boxes are used in the house or studio, nothing else is needed to make them excellent pieces of equipment. If you plan to use them outdoors or in an unheated building, greenware or supplies can be protected from freezing weather by inserting a lighted bulb in the box.

**Convert typical steel utility shelving** for more versatile studio use: Purchase the shelving unassembled, and when joining the posts to the shelf, attach the latter upside down. The shelf now is a heavy frame with an inch-deep recess. Once the air spaces and screw holes have been blocked with clay, wet plaster can be poured to fill each shelf cavity.

Wrap heavy-gauge, plastic sheet between one or two of these plaster-filled shelves, wet them, and use this as a damp box. Other plaster shelves can be used to dry clay, while hard-to-reach shelves can be assembled in the usual manner and used for storage.

**Achieve proper storage** or drying control with a set of shelves deep and wide enough to accept wheel head bats. The shelves are constructed of ⅝-inch particleboard between vertical particleboard sides. The bottom shelf is 3 inches up from the floor, and the top rests on, rather than cutting between, the sides. A ¼-inch plywood backing should be used to provide bracing independent of the wall and close the box for moisture control. The front of the shelves is draped with an inexpensive clear plastic drop cloth, either loosely or tightly, as the situation requires. To hold ware fresh for further work, the plastic is tucked in at the bottom and pulled tightly at the sides. For controlled drying, the plastic is loosened, depending on the humidity/weather.

**The form** used in making a catenary kiln arch can be converted into an excellent damp box when lined with plastic garbage bags and fitted with adjustable shelves. The door can be made by sawing a section out of the front of the form and attaching hinges to it. The damp box will never be too small to accommodate your largest fireable objects.

**Empty 2- and 3-gallon plastic** ice cream containers can be used for storage of ceramic projects. They stack nicely and conserve space in small studios.

**Use Styrofoam picnic coolers** as "damp rooms" by inverting the container over pots after taking them off the wheel.

**Old plastic shower curtains** and tablecloths, purchased from thrift shops, make inexpensive covering for a damp box made of $2 \times 4$s.

## Grinders

**A grinding wheel** for smoothing the bottoms of finished pottery can be improvised by using some sandpaper, slip and the potter's wheel. Simply cut out a round piece of sandpaper, smear the back side of it with a thick slip and press this down on the center of the wheel head to fasten it. It is surprising what a good job this does when the wheel is rotated rapidly. The sandpaper holds very well and it is easily removed, too.

**To facilitate massive grinding jobs** such as leveling a chipped foot rim or removing glaze which has run onto the base of a pot, dismantle your grinding wheel, center the disk on the potter's wheel, and fasten it in place with clay (as if it were a bat). As the wheel rotates at high speed, hold the base of the pot firmly against the grinding surface until the desired results are obtained. The process should be suitable for electric as well as kickwheels.

**Any electric wheel** with a Masonite or particleboard bat-and-pin system can be a heavy-duty grinder for cleaning kiln wash off pot bottoms. Car body sanding disks can be purchased cheaply in many sizes or grades, and glued with contact cement onto a bat, which can then be put on the wheel as needed. If the disk gets clogged, a toothbrush will clean it while spinning.

**For an inexpensive but effective grinder,** position a broken piece of silicon carbide kiln shelf on a wooden bat and then secure it in place using pieces of scrap plywood nailed to the bat around the edges of the kiln shelf. The bat is then attached to the head of a potter's wheel. Apply a few drops of oil to the surface of the kiln shelf and rotate the wheel as if centering. The spinning kiln shelf will beautifully grind and polish the rough clay or glaze surfaces. *Caution:* the wooden bat must be firmly attached to the wheel head. A poorly fastened bat or kiln shelf can cause injury. Clay should not be used for fastening because it may not hold the bat or kiln shelf in place.

**To remove unwanted glaze** from the bottom of pots, apply to the foot a paste consisting of fine silicon carbide (FFF) and water. Twist this against the bottom of another form, adding water as needed. The result will be a smooth finish on both objects which won't scratch other surfaces.

The technique also works on individual tight-fitting lids, which can be made to fit more loosely by adding the paste and turning the lid around in its seating rim until it is sufficiently ground smooth.

**An old electric knife sharpener,** with part of the casing removed, works fairly well as a grinding wheel for hard-to-reach spots on pot bottoms where glaze has dripped down during firing, or for out-of-the-way rough edges

**A masonry saw blade,** mounted on the arbor of a ¼-horsepower motor, cleans the bases of glaze-fired ware efficiently.

## Scales

**A beam scale** or two-pan laboratory balance should never be read with the pointer resting at zero. No matter how well the knife edge pivots, there always is a little friction which can introduce an error of 0.1 to 0.2 grams. This can be significant when weighing small samples, especially the coloring oxides where small differences in amounts can have a large impact on the final color of the glaze.

The correct way to use a balance is to have it in motion at all times. Correct weight is obtained when the pointer makes equal excursions on either side of the zero mark. This, incidentally, is the purpose of the graduations on either side of zero on the pointer index.

**For potters who economized** by not buying the scoop-shaped pan for their triple beam balance and use household pans instead, but have spent hours looking for accurate counterbalance weights, brad or tack containers make excellent weights. Each one has a cap with a tab for hanging. Simply fill one with sand until the total weight balances a corresponding pan, then mark both for identification. Be sure to hang the weight in the same notch on the balance each time it is used.

**Try keeping scales handy** and dust-free under a plastic toaster cover. These covers are available in most supermarket and department stores, and come in a standard size which will fit most scales. If the cover is a bit too tall, a strip can be cut from the bottom.

## Spray Booths and Sprayers

**Instead of giving** your old clothes dryer to the junkman, remove the front panel of the machine and strip most of the interior, leaving only the exhaust fan and motor. Then build a stand 30 inches tall from 2×4s, and add a plywood shelf to hold the compressor and any other equipment or supplies related to spraying. (The stand can be nailed together, although wood screws are preferred because vibration from the compressor may eventually loosen nails.) The spray booth area of a typical dryer measures 30×30 inches across the front, and 20 inches deep—plenty of space for most spraying jobs. Use the existing, built-in exhaust fan to vent the air from the spray booth out of the studio. Before using glaze, you may want to spray paint the whole unit.

**For an inexpensive spray booth,** cut a dry cleaner's plastic bag along one side and at the end; suspend from the ceiling with a metal hoop, then add a simple turntable inside, placed on a plastic cloth. Overspray may be reclaimed fairly easily when dry.

**An energy-efficient** means of spraying glaze is to use an old-fashioned flit gun (a hand pump sprayer for insecticides). Fill it with glaze thinned to a suitable consistency.

**A plant mister** may serve as an air-free sprayer for glazes and stains. First, remove the fine-intake sieve which will easily clog, then fill with a rather fluid mixture. It may be advisable to experiment with different misters, as some may contain materials that electrostatically collect fine particles, and others are more easily disassembled for cleaning.

**An empty towelettes** pop-up dispenser makes an inexpensive and convenient spray-glaze container. The tight slits at the top hold a sprayer securely while the closed lid stops any spillage of glaze.

**For spraying glazes,** excellent results may be obtained with a combination of a garden-type pressure sprayer and the top of a hand-operated pump sprayer. Remove the hand pump from the sprayer unit and connect the hose from the pressure sprayer to the place where the hand pump had been. The self-closing valve of the garden spray hose serves for the operation of this sprayer.

To operate, don't place any liquid in the garden sprayer, but pump up the pressure as usual and operate the valve to spray. This gives a very even coating of glaze, even if the glaze is of a rich, creamy consistency.

**Experimentation** resulted in a much less expensive alternative glaze sprayer that works quite well. Instead of an air compressor, it uses a vacuum cleaner with the hose plugged into the exhaust port to create an air stream. The hose nozzle is inserted into one end of a 1⅛-inch diameter galvanized T fitting and the stream of air is reduced down

(with a succession of pipe fittings) to ⅜-inch diameter at the other end. (The vacuum cleaner produces lower air pressure than a compressor, so a large spray orifice in the ⅜-inch range is needed to achieve the same atomizing effect.) A length of plastic tube from the inside of a discarded spray can works well, and the stream of air across the mouth of this tube will draw up both slip and glaze from inside a jar, misting them at the point of convergence. Instead of a "trigger" to activate the gun, just place your hand over the open orifice on top of the T to divert the airstream through the ⅜-inch nozzle. The gun will only spray when all the air is diverted through the nozzle, so the vacuum cleaner can be left running without worrying about unintentional spraying. Assuming you already have a suitable vacuum cleaner and an empty jar, the whole thing costs very little and can be assembled in about an hour.

**The Kirby Company** makes a spray gun attachment especially for use with the exhaust end of a vacuum cleaner. The spray gun features a trigger control and a coarse-to-fine spray adjustment; it accepts standard pint or quart canning jars, and can be attached to almost any studio shop vacuum with a simple hose coupling. It may be necessary to experiment with the siphon tube diameter for the type of material to be sprayed; try inserting a piece of 12-gauge wire insulation for oxides. The front ½ inch of the barrel may be sawed off where it extends beyond the nozzle to prevent dripping and guard against the collection of spray.

## Ware Racks and Boards

**Discarded refrigerator shelves** or racks make excellent drying racks for the ceramist. Because they are of "open" construction they permit air to circulate underneath works that are put on them, and assure more even drying. Another advantage is that they are strong and rigid and will hold even heavy forms without any danger of collapsing.

**L-shaped metal shelf brackets** (obtainable in hardware stores) make strong, easily installed ware board racks; they can be fastened directly to a vertical wall at regular intervals to support the ends of equal-length boards. For installation in the middle of a room or in the case of a sloping attic wall, they can be screwed into either side of a vertical 2 × 4-inch stud. A small piece of plywood may be secured on top of each bracket for additional width when supporting the ends of two ware boards.

**Cafeteria trays** make excellent, lightweight, nonwarping ware boards. These are sturdy, water-resistant, easy to clean, and stack when not in use.

# Wedging Boards and Surfaces

**To construct** a good wedging surface, purchase a printer's blanket (available from industrial printing supply firms) and nail it reverse side up on a wood backing. The porous blanket is absorbent and easy to clean, yet does not chip like plaster.

**Tack several flaps** of canvas across the rear of the wedging board. As you change from one color of clay to another, just flip to the appropriate canvas. This system also protects the plaster surface and prevents contamination of the clay.

**A pastry canvas** (available in the houseware section of many department stores) is a useful, portable wedging surface. It has wooden slats on opposite ends and two metal rods that support them. Either of the slats hook over the edge of a table to secure the canvas, which can be folded for storage. It usually comes with a rolling pin "sock" which provides an interesting texture for clay slabs.

**A satisfactory wedging board** can be made by cutting down the sides of a strong corrugated cardboard carton to an inch or so above its base and filling it with plaster. The cardboard sticks to the plaster and becomes its permanent frame. It is resilient enough to cushion the wedging blows so that even a relatively thin base beneath can withstand the wedging impact.

**A small portable wedging board** can easily be made by reinforcing a shallow fruit box and filling it with a good plaster mix. The wooden box will give you a permanent support for your block of plaster, enabling you to move it or store it without the danger of having it crack. For use, it can be easily secured to a work table with a C clamp.

**You can make** a convenient wedging bench simply by installing a vise on a table, placing an eye lag screw into the wall and attaching baling wire between the two. The wire can be wrapped about the jaw of the vise and given a turn or two about itself. To get tension simply screw the vise out until the wire is as taut as desired. Wedging can be done on the work bench if a square of canvas is stretched and fastened over the working surface. When the wire is not needed for wedging, it can be unwound from the vise jaw and allowed to hang from the eye bolt, thus freeing the vise for normal use.

A **wedging wire** that is stretched too tightly is more likely to snap under the pressure of hard use than one that is left just a little bit slack. There also is less chance that someone may possibly be injured by a piece of broken wire. If the wire is fastened to the wedging bench with a turnbuckle arrangement, it is a simple matter to loosen the wire to the degree of tautness desired; if the wire is permanently fixed in place, it should be given just a little bit of "play" when it is fastened.

**Stainless steel leader wire,** used in fishing, is an excellent, long-lived material for a good wedging wire.

**A guitar E-string** makes an excellent wedging wire. It is strong, will not rust, and is easy to attach.

**Try using nylon string** from a tennis racket as a virtually indestructible wire for your wedging table. Check a tennis pro shop for scrap pieces from broken rackets.

**For an inexpensive wedging board,** nail a section of particleboard on top of an old dresser or any sturdy table. Particleboard is available in lumber and building supply stores, and is made from sawdust, wood scraps and glue. Any leftover can be used for shelving.

**Top quality pool tables** are usually made of three pieces of slate 2½ × 4 feet or larger, and up to 2 inches thick. Slate that is flawed, or otherwise unfit for use in these tables, can often be obtained free from shops which make and repair them. Slate slabs are easily cut and drilled, and when set on bricks or other sturdy frames, make admirable surfaces on which to work clay.

**Make a wedging board** of Portland cement. The base (under part) should be a 3 to 1 mix and the top ⅛-inch neat cement. This is troweled smooth and the top edges beveled.
A cement wedging board doesn't need a "frame" around it for support. It can be poured in a cardboard box, the cardboard to be torn away later. For real sturdiness and weight, you can cast it in a wooden soft-drink box.

**Place a smooth concrete slab** just outdoors from your studio to wedge and dry out wet clay on warm days. The heat absorbed by the slab removes unwanted moisture quickly.

## Wheels and Accessories

**For slowing the momentum** of a heavy concrete flywheel, fit your kick wheel with a device which utilizes a section of old tire as a friction brake. A strip of the rubber is nailed over one end of a short section of $2 \times 4$ lumber; then the other end of the wood is equipped with a heavy-duty hinge, bolted to the frame of the wheel at an appropriate height above the flywheel so that the brake can be brought down to a diagonal position for braking. A spring and a length of wire, secured between two screw eyes (one on the upper surface of the $2 \times 4$ and another attached to the frame of the wheel) keep the brake retracted when not in use.

**Use a practice hockey puck** as an inexpensive friction driver for a motorized kick wheel. A ¼-inch hole drilled in the center of the disk accommodates the motor shaft. Being made of soft spongy rubber, the puck has lots of grip, and as it wears down to a cone shape, it works even better.

**When throwing** on a kick wheel propelled by a metal or wood flywheel, there is often a tendency for the foot to slip as clay and water find their way to the traction surface. A good solution is to apply several stick-on shower or bath appliques to the flywheel, providing a secure grip even when wet.

**If you plan to build** a wheel from a kit, money can be saved by substituting for the optional drip pan a large round cake pan available from a restaurant supply company. It is less expensive and serves the same purpose. And, to cut costs even more, you can make your own flywheel. A regular size portable barbecue grill, $24 \times 3$ inches, is perfect for a mold. Filling this with concrete produces a flywheel weighing at least 120 pounds.

**Build a piggy-back electric drive** for a kick wheel in an arrangement similar to the Randall power attachment. The two-speed motor from a worn-out automatic washer may be installed at a low cost for the friction-drive wheel, studio wiring, boxes, switches and miscellaneous materials. Both speeds are useful, which surely saves effort.

**If your thrown pots** consistently develop a bulge or thin spot in approximately the same place on each pot, check your wheel to see if it is level.

**An inexpensive, removable splash pan** adaptable to any wheel with a deck can be constructed from a round section cut from a Formica-topped counter. Such a shape can sometimes be obtained from lumberyards or kitchen and bath remodelers as scrap, when sink openings are cut in countertops. The circle should be 18 inches in diameter and cut in half after drilling or cutting a 2⅛-inch centered hole.

The splash pan rim is formed from a 4½-inch-wide strip, cut from the top of a plastic garbage can. Place one end of the

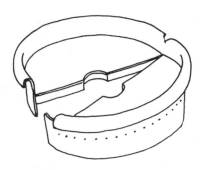

strip against the curved side of one of the semicircles, and tack it down. Put both halves of the circle together and continue tacking. The excess may be tucked under, forming a more secure connection when the splash pan is closed around the wheel head. Before using the pan, its seam can be sealed with bathtub caulking.

**To facilitate cleanup** for a Randall wheel, drill a ⅜-inch hole near the base of the splash pan and plug it with a cork from the outside. The cork can be removed to collect the slurry in a bucket for reuse. Solid pieces of clay can then be removed by hand with less mess.

**A baby's plastic bathtub** makes a sturdy, easily cleaned splash pan for your wheel, and the cost is minimal.

**If you don't have a splash pan** on your wheel, wrap 1-inch-wide masking tape around the wheel head, leaving about ½ inch above the throwing surface. This border prevents drainage of slip until you are ready to sponge it up.

**Should the plastic pan** on your electric wheel crack, patch it with PVC cement. This colorless adhesive is available at hard-

118

ware stores or plumbing supply places and is used to cement plastic water lines, so it works great on the hard plastic pans.

**A sponge,** tied to the water bowl and lined up with the edge of the wheel head, absorbs almost all the excess water produced. Simply attach the sponge to the bowl with a rubberband so that the sponge gently touches the edge and top of the wheel head, preventing the splashing of slip or water.

**To protect the on/off switch** of an electric wheel, cut off the neck of an ordinary size balloon and stretch the remainder over the switch. A balloon lasts four or five months and allows use even when hands are wet or covered with clay.

## Miscellaneous Studio Aids

**Instead of pulling** your back out by tugging a garbage can of clay from place to place, convert an old rotary power mower to a useful hauler. Undo the bolts holding the engine and remove it; then place the clay can directly on the frame. It handles like a shopping cart.

**One of the greatest conveniences** one can have in the studio is a small table on rollers. A used typing table may be purchased very cheaply for stacking ware that must be moved from one place to another in the studio. It is especially convenient for loading the kiln and can save many extra trips across the room.

**An inexpensive and versatile** drain trap for utility sinks can be easily constructed from a plastic bucket with a snap-on lid that seals tightly. These are usually available from donut shops or other food distributors.

A plastic compression sleeve is cut in two, and half is mounted on the lid with plastic cement; the other half is adhered to one side of the bucket. With proper registration to existing pipes, this completed unit replaces the U trap that is usually installed. The bucket can be easily removed to empty accumulated debris that might otherwise clog the plumbing.

For an efficient fringe benefit, the trap can be removed to catch materials in another container when pouring slip or glazes on ware at the sink. (See "An Inexpensive Studio Sink Trap," by Ric Swenson, in the December '78 CM for a more elaborate version of this idea.)

119

**The operating room** of a local hospital may be a source for used equipment, such as various sizes of rubber and plastic syringes (useful for glaze and slip trailing), combination sponge/fingernail scrubbers and 6-foot lengths of two-wire electric cord that can be made into extension cords. A hospital uses these items once and then they are tossed out because it is too expensive to sterilize them again.

**Inexpensive raku tongs** can be fabricated by welding two 2-foot lengths of ½-inch steel rod to the jaws of a pair of pliers. The grips of the pliers thus become the grasping portion of the tongs, while the rods serve as handles.

**Flat storage turntables** sold in department and variety stores for use in kitchen cabinets are far less expensive than those made specifically for ceramic work, and they have several advantages such as their light weight (but will still hold and revolve under quite heavy objects). In addition, they are easy to clean, easy to store and are readily available.

**Recycle an old record turntable** as a banding wheel for applying slips and wax resist. The speed of the turntable can be changed to accommodate various sizes of pots.

**A lawn roller** makes an excellent clay crusher.

**An old gun-type hair dryer** and an old goose-neck lamp or desk lamp with tension arm can be combined to make a convenient pot dryer. Remove the bulb and shade and attach the dryer (one method employs wire and a hot glue gun). Screw the base of the lamp to a table or wall so the dryer can be pulled down or across to the object being dried on the wheel head. The dryer can be pushed out of the way when not in use.

**The Giffin Grip,** designed as a footing aid, is also helpful for holding Masonite throwing bats, particularly smaller ones (6–8 inches in diameter) which will not reach the wheel head keys.

**Convert a tin pie plate** to a pair of pot lifters by cutting it in half with an X-acto knife. The plates available in grocery and hardware stores are usually too lightweight for this purpose, so it is best to obtain the heavy-duty type used in commercial bakeries.

**A no-cost glaze mixer** can be made from materials easily found around the studio. Place a bucket of dry glaze materials on the potter's wheel, and mix the ingredients with a wooden spoon while the wheel rotates. Add the proper amount of water and repeat.

**An old-fashioned washing machine** with wringers can be purchased cheaply at swap meets and converted into a slab roller, with just a few minor adjustments. First, detach the bar which connects the motor to the barrel—this will stop the washing machine from working, while allowing the wringer to run freely. Add a piece of wood between the rollers in the wringer to adjust clay thickness.

**Here is a quick** and ideal method for making slabs by use of an old mangle (ironing machine). A flat board is used as a base plate, and this will roll through the mangle (1). Cloth is placed

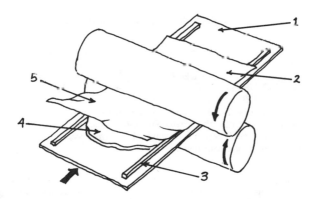

on the surface of the board (2). Sticks for the required thickness of clay are placed on both outer edges of the surface board (3). Clay is wedged and slightly flattened, then it is placed between the sticks (4). Another cloth is placed over the clay to prevent it from sticking to the rollers (5).

As the rollers are rotated, the clay is drawn through the mangle and flattened to the thickness of the sticks. This results in an even slab that is free of air bubbles. There should be no trouble with warping, and cracking only occurs if the cloth doubles up under the rollers and leaves a line impressed in the clay.

# Kilns

## Kilnbuilding

**No matter how well you plan** the opening for a stacked brick kiln door, there always seems to be less than a perfect fit. Solve this problem by including two wedge-shaped bricks in each course laid as door bricks. The farther in the protruding wedge is pushed, the tighter the row of bricks becomes.

**On some sprung arch salt kilns** it is necessary to cut brick to fill in the gap where the inside curve of the arch and the straight edge of the bricked-up door don't meet. An alternate solution is to make a form which corresponds to the thickness and size of the curved gap, and fill it with high-heat-resistant refractory castable. Bend an iron rod into the shape of a handle and put it into the form. Now each time the bricks of the kiln door are stacked and unstacked the top may be pulled out or put in in one uniform piece.

**A good place** to obtain inexpensive firebrick is the local power company. They often rebuild or take down boilers, or have a surplus of refractory materials. The used brick is suitable for kilnbuilding and firing at stoneware temperatures.

**After completing the walls** of a kiln from a hodgepodge of broken soft bricks, it may be necessary to even the inner surface. A tool for this purpose may be formed from a large, 46-ounce juice can, its ends removed and the container opened flat. After punching the can full of holes with a 16-penny nail to form a rough, jagged surface, nail it to a short length of $2 \times 4$ lumber. The resulting rasp will not clog and can be used to shape soft brick for kiln door arches, etc., with ease.

**For easy removal** of an arch form when constructing a kiln, base the form on a 3-inch-thick slab of firm foam rubber. When the brick is in place, the arch template can easily be removed by pressing it down slightly into the foam.

**Instructions for designing** a catenary arch kiln usually suggest that you trace a string or chain suspended between two points on a vertical surface. This method is time-consuming and somewhat difficult because the string or chain moves as the pencil line is drawn. It is easier to spray the hanging string with aerosol paint; when the string is removed a perfect image remains.

**A kiln that serves well** for firing items or for testing clay and glazes can be made from an empty 3-pound coffee can. It should reach a temperature of 1500°F in about 30 minutes. The inside of the can is lined with Fiberfrax Lo-Con brand insulating ceramic fiber (made by the Carborundum Co., Refractories and Electronics Division, Box 367, Niagara Falls, N.Y. 14302), which is then folded and tied to the outside surface with wire. The can is inverted to its firing position and a peephole is cut through the top of the inverted can and its fiber lining. Then a square of fiber is cut to lay over the hole. Another hole is cut for a pyrometer, and the insulated can is set over a heating element from a hot plate. The kiln is placed on four insulating firebricks, and fired. When the ware has completed its firing cycle, the coffee can is lifted from the hot plate. This kiln is also great for demonstrating raku.

**An excellent** gas-fired, updraft, raku kiln can be made from an old, broken, top-loading electric kiln. Cut holes in the sides for burners and flue, then mount the kiln to fire on its side with the lid hinge to the right or left. Front loading is easier and safer for raku firing. This kiln might also substitute for stoneware and bisque firings.

**One-inch-thick refractory** fiber insulation in rigid board form makes an easily cut-to-fit, lightweight, and relatively cool damper for the kiln. While it should be protected from dampness, it may be air dried after accidental exposure to rain and still perform well.

**For an inexpensive downdraft** kiln chimney, obtain empty 16-gallon drums (used to transport rustproofing compound) from auto rustproofing companies. Cut out both ends and tack-weld together as many as required to obtain the desired height. Such a chimney is very light, can easily be installed by one person, is essentially free and will last about a year before rusting through.

**A large round** outdoor metal barbecue grill, inverted and fitted with stovepipe, makes an efficient hood for collecting and venting exhaust gases from an updraft kiln. Remove the legs of the grill, cut a hole in the center of the metal pan, and attach a length of stovepipe long enough to extend through the roof of the kiln shed. The hood can then be suspended over the flue with lengths of chain, attached to ceiling beams or other structural supports.

**Owners of octagon** or decagon top-loading electric kilns can easily increase the height of the firing chamber. Rather than buy the 4½-inch blank collar listed by most dealers, purchase, instead, eight or ten firebricks. For the octagon, miter each end to 22½°, and for the decagon, 18°. Remove the hinge pin and set the lid down on the row of bricks. This gives the same increase in height at less than one-third the cost, and if joints are carefully cut, heat loss remains minimal.

# Burners

**A wad** of old wire elements from an electric kiln, packed into the firing tip of a noncommercially made burner, helps prevent backburning.

**Discarded water heaters** and home furnaces are a source for inexpensive atmospheric burners adaptable for equipping kilns. Once the deflector plates are removed with a hacksaw, water heater burners can be fitted individually in portable raku kilns, or paired in groups of four to eight for larger chambers. These are often available at junkyards for a cost equal to the salvage value of the metal. Used home furnace burners, some as large as 100,000 to 200,000 Btu's, are sometimes available from local installers at nominal cost or free of charge.

**Many potters** use homemade burners or weed burners without a safety pilot, particularly when firing a raku kiln. This may require turning up the burner slowly and watching the flame carefully so it does not blow out in the early stages of firing. A glowing brick directly in the flame path (called an ignition brick) will keep the burner lit eventually, when sufficiently hot. But by placing one or two charcoal briquettes at the base of the ignition brick, the flame may be turned up much faster, preventing flameout. It takes only a few minutes for the briquettes to ignite. They last long enough to keep the flame lit until the ignition brick gets red hot and takes over.

**A very good kiln pilot** can be made from the burner of a propane soldering torch. First, remove the tip and tube (which comprise the burner) from the valve which goes into the propane cylinder. This may now be adapted to screw into a standard gas valve purchased from any hardware store. Second, drill the orifice to approximately 1/16-inch diameter. Permanently plumb the burner to your system. With these pilots, a small kiln can be fired to 1000°F before turning on the main burners.

## Elements

**Try the following technique** for winding Kanthal replacement elements for your electric kiln: Obtain a section of steel rod approximately 6 inches longer than the desired length of coil; rod diameter should correspond to the internal diameter of the element. Hold the rod vertically and place one end in the center of the head of your potter's wheel. Grip the end resting on the wheel head in a pair of Vise-Grips (a type of locking pliers sold in most hardware stores), then secure both rod base and tool in the centered position by firmly pressing several pounds of clay over them. As the wheel is rotated, the free end of the rod is steadied with one hand, while the element wire is spiraled around the rod. If difficulty is encountered in attaching the wire for the first few turns, try embedding it in the clay or securing it to the handles of the Vise-Grips before covering them with clay. The coiled element can easily be removed from the rod by turning it slightly in the opposite direction to which it was wound.

**Concerning the control** of temperature rise in a self-wired electric kiln, there are at least two inexpensive answers. First, you could (provided the kiln draws 4000 watts or less) obtain an infinite heat switch—the type used on the surface burner of an electric range. This switch will work, although overloaded at near 4000 watts, and a new one should be available at appliance repair shops. A second solution is to install a double pole, double throw, knife switch (the porcelain base type). This switch is available at most hardware stores. The kiln can then be started on 118 volt power, and switched to 236 volts when more heat is needed.

**When working element wire** through a hole in a softbrick, electric-kiln wall, the job goes much faster if you first insert a plastic drinking straw through the hole from the outside until visible inside. Slide the wire lead of the element into the straw and through the wall, then remove the straw.

## Kiln Care and Cleaning

**Always use a vacuum cleaner** inside your kiln before each firing. This will remove all loose particles of refractory brick and so prevent them from landing on and ruining the ware being glazed.

**To keep the exterior** metal parts of your electric kiln shiny, use any standard brand of toothpaste as polish.

**To remove rust** from kiln hinges and other metal areas of the kiln, use a bit of dry glaze or thick, mixed, clear glaze on a scrap of terry cloth and rub well.

**An ordinary meat baster** is very useful for cleaning out any particles of crumbled porous firebrick or any other materials that become lodged in the spy hole of the kiln. If one blows his breath into the kiln to clear the atmosphere so that the cones can be better seen, there is always a chance that some of this material might be blown onto a piece of glazed ware and permanently mar its surface. The meat baster can be used to blow the loose particles from the inside toward the outside just before the kiln is fired.

**The top edges of the kiln** and the edges of the kiln lid are subjected to especially hard wear, and these are the first areas that show a tendency to deteriorate and crumble. You can avoid this by applying a thin smear of good kiln cement (not kiln wash) to these and any other exposed areas. First dampen a small area of the kiln top thoroughly with a sopping sponge, then smear on the cement and smooth it with the wet sponge. Continue this procedure with the other areas until the job is done. Allow the cement to dry, with the lid open, for 24 hours. Brush the worked-on areas to remove loose particles and then use a vacuum cleaner to remove the crumbs from within the kiln.

**Over a period of years,** many top-loading kilns are unnecessarily damaged by objects falling on their lids, by using the kiln lid as a tabletop, or other abuse. A disk of ¾-inch plywood, cut the diameter of your kiln lid, can be placed on the kiln whenever it is cool, and can even serve as a worktable. In smaller studio spaces, the resulting additional workspace, or storage space, can be significant. With the high price of replacement lids, this plywood protection is well worth the effort, adding years to kiln life.

## Kiln Furniture

**Store scraps** and odd bits of clay until a sizable quantity has accumulated. Then, add about one-third grog and use this mixture to make posts and small shelves, which after firing should prove to be excellent space savers in the kiln.

**When loading the kiln,** time is often lost locating a post of the appropriate height to complete the setting of a shelf, especially when posts are relatively close in height. Use an oxide wash to paint the height in inches on each face of your kiln shelf post. After one firing, the numbers are permanent and you will never have to guess the size again.

**Keep kiln posts** tied together with an elastic band in groups of three or four of the same length. You can save time when stacking a kiln if you don't have to hunt through a box full of posts of mixed sizes.

**A holder for kiln posts** can be a real time saver when you're loading the kiln. Use a $12 \times 36 \times \frac{1}{2}$-inch board and nail large finishing nails (headless nails) in at an angle, spacing them about 2 inches apart. The holder may be hung on the wall near the kiln, and the posts placed on the nails.

**Don't throw away** those broken kiln shelves. Break up the larger chunks into pieces 1 inch square or slightly larger. Then grind off all traces of old kiln wash and glaze, smooth off rough and flaking exposed cracked surfaces and corners, and you have some very useful pieces of kiln furniture that are of uniform thickness. These can be used as spacer tiles to increase the height of a shelf that needs just half an inch or so.

## Kiln Moving

**Recently my stoneware kiln was moved** to a new location 13 miles away. Cutting the steel and sawing the mortared softbrick into sections seemed the only way to accomplish the goal, but after talking to a very inventive house mover, it was moved in one piece.

The kiln is a 45-cubic-foot downdraft, sitting on $8 \times 8 \times 16$-inch concrete blocks on a concrete slab. The two-layer floor and the first three layers of the walls are hardbrick, as well as the entire chimney; the remainder of the walls and the arch are K-23 softbrick. All four corners are wrapped with angle iron and hinged permanently, and the chimney extension is a 10-foot section of 10-inch-diameter steel culvert.

Two-inch steel pipe was inserted through the holes in the concrete blocks and common sections were welded across both ends of the pipes; large (30-ton) hydraulic jacks raised the kiln high enough to place a pair of axles in back and to attach a

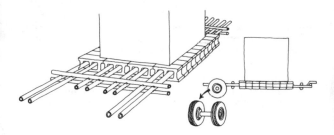

trailer hitch in front, giving, in essence, a kiln on wheels. The raising had to be done very slowly and evenly; the concrete blocks shifted a bit, but a few well-placed shims firmed up the structure. Once the kiln was in the air on its new-found wheels, a bit of maneuvering was necessary to remove it from within the shed.

Pulling it to its new location required further finesse because of its low clearance; top speed for the trip was 27 miles per hour, with an average of about 15 miles per hour.

**Anyone contemplating building** a "permanent" kiln should look ahead to a time when nevertheless it may require moving. Always frame the base perimeter with adequate angle iron (legs inside) and place a heavy steel plate inside the base frame prior to building. With lifting lugs welded or bolted to each of the four corners, the mechanics of moving it will be greatly simplified. Aside from floor support, the steel plate also acts as a seal against moisture absorption.

## Repairs

**If caught without a spare element** for an electric kiln, carefully encircle the two broken ends and squeeze a ball of wet clay around this joint. The kiln is fired using the remaining two elements first, and then turning the patched element on. The clay shrinks upon firing and should provide good contact, allowing the element to work. This can be successful through as many as three additional firings.

**Sometimes the elements** in an electric kiln sag out of the insulating brick grooves after repeated firings. To put them back without breaking the brittle metal coils, heat the sagging area with a blow torch until red hot, and then push the element back into the groove. If the firebrick groove is sufficiently damaged, the coil can be pinned in place in the usual manner.

**A high-temperature cement** that is effective to 2700°F (1500°C) may be made by mixing talc with liquid sodium silicate to any consistency—a thin paste, putty or in between. It's ideal for repairing shelves and shelf posts, or gluing pins in electric kilns to hold resistance wire in place. It also makes an excellent ceramic-to-metal adhesive.

**To repair damaged kiln furniture,** prepare a mixture of one part each of ball clay, kaolin, flint and feldspar then blend into a paste with sodium silicate. The broken piece is mended with this paste, allowed to dry and then fired.

**To repair cracks** in the firebrick lining on the inside of a kiln, use a mortar made from ground-up firebrick and clay slip. First, crush or grind pieces of the porous firebrick with mortar and pestle, enough to fill all of the cracks. Next, add a minimum amount of clay slip to form a mortar consistency.

(The slip must have a maturing temperature commensurate with your usual firing ranges.) Mix well and press the mortar into the cracks. The kiln can be fired when the mortar is dry.

**When repairing** the insulating firebrick in kilns, it is necessary to wet thoroughly the area to be repaired before applying the high-temperature cement. Sometimes this is very difficult to do, especially in hard-to-reach places in small kilns.

A bulb-type slip-trailing syringe is an excellent device for squirting the water just where it is needed. It may also be used to squirt thinned high-temperature cement into hard-to-reach places.

**Damaged kiln furniture** can be made serviceable again if the broken pieces are joined with a paste of high-fire glaze, and fired in an upright position.

## Kiln Shelves

**Since mullite shelves bend** after several Cone 10 firings, try eliminating kiln wash and turning the shelves over before each firing. If you know your glazes and use an adequate dry foot, this method is a great money saver.

**Old, built-up kiln wash** can be removed rather easily with an electric belt sander (use a 3-inch or wider belt of no. 60 aluminum oxide or silicon carbide grit). If the sander is properly handled, glaze beads will be ground off flush with the original surface of the shelf. Furthermore, kiln wash in indentations on the shelf will be sanded flush with the shelf surface. The speed with which the tool works makes renting a sander worthwhile, if one is not accessible otherwise.

**After firing a glaze kiln,** cover shelf surfaces with a damp cloth for a period of time before attempting to remove drips and splatters with the traditional chisel and mallet. This allows the glaze and kiln wash to be removed without chipping the actual shelf surface.

**In order to remove** old kiln wash from kiln shelves, soak the shelves in water for a day or two. Then use a putty knife and nearly all of the old kiln wash will scrape off. Any stubborn spots can be removed easily on a grinding wheel.

**When kiln wash builds up** on shelves, producing a rough, uneven surface, it can be sanded smooth with a section of hard firebrick.

**In a studio** where several people use the kiln, shelves become a mess with kiln wash and glaze runs. For a small fee, a monument company may be able to clean a number of shelves with carbide blasting. The surfaces will be somewhat more rough than when new, but excellent for applications of new kiln wash.

**Wafer-thin slabs** of your standard clay body, laced generously with fireclay and dusted with flint, make excellent setter tiles for protecting shelves from overly fluid glazes. In England, these clay pads are called biscuits.

## Kiln Wash

**Before applying wash** (half kaolin, half 200-mesh flint) to new kiln shelves, dip the whole shelf in water for a few seconds; this will help the wash sink deeper into the surface. Additionally, if the kiln wash is cracking or curling during firing, remix it with an increased amount of flint (40 parts kaolin to 60 parts or more flint).

**An easy method** for applying kiln wash to shelves is to use a paint roller and pan. One coat leaves a smooth and even surface.

**By placing kiln wash** in a spray gun and spraying it on, it is easier to get the desired thickness, and the surface is much smoother.

**An excellent applicator** for kiln wash is an ordinary cellulose sponge that is first dampened with water. Squeezing the sponge after dipping it in the kiln wash allows a very even (heavy or light) application. Also, this same sponge is ideal to "brush off" any foreign material from the top, edges and bottom of shelves, when loading the kiln, or to remove loose, flaking kiln wash. This will prevent raking your hand over a protruding piece of glaze you can't see and perhaps getting a nasty cut. You can feel a sharp piece of old glaze on the shelf with the sponge, something you can't do with a brush.

**A wide whitewash-type brush** is useful for spreading the kiln wash in an even layer on the shelves. If you have made the kiln wash too thin and are having trouble getting a heavy coat on the shelves, try heating the shelves slightly just before coating them.

**Mix some epsom salts** with kiln wash and it flows on like plastic paint. It takes a bit longer to dry, but is worth it.

**Adding about 2% bentonite** to the dry kiln wash before the water is added not only prevents the materials from settling to the bottom of the container, but offers a better bond when the wash is applied to the kiln shelves.

**To keep kiln shelves** and the kiln floor in good condition: Save an empty squirt container that held a dishwashing detergent. Fill this with a medium-to-heavy solution of kiln wash and keep it near the kiln. When glaze drippings adhere to shelves or floor, merely chip them off in the usual manner and then squirt some kiln wash from the dispenser onto the offending spots. Shake the container before using and hold a finger over the opening.

If the kiln wash in the dispenser should dry out eventually, open the bottle by removing the cap, add a little water, close and then shake. You are back in business with a minimum of effort.

**Instead of placing pots** on kiln wash alone, mix the wash in the usual manner, but thicker and applied heavily with a large brush. Before the kiln wash dries, a generous layer of fine sil-

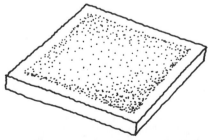

ica sand is spread over the shelf, leaving a small margin so no sand will fall off. Ware may be placed on the shelf immediately. After the glaze firing, the pots are easily lifted off the shelf, and the sand is smoothed again for subsequent use.

**Adding gum solution** to kiln wash prevents it from cracking and chipping off the shelf before firing.

**The conventional mix** of 50% kaolin, 50% flint as kiln wash has a tendency to chip and peel. This is probably because of the low dry strength of kaolin, and its lack of bond with the flint. A good mix is 50% flint, 25% kaolin and 25% Cedar Heights Goldart Clay or A.P. Green Fireclay, the latter sifted through a 40-mesh screen to eliminate coarse particles which make a smooth coating difficult. This mixture holds well at Cone 9, gives no lifting or peeling problems, and is relatively easy to remove when glaze flows onto it. It may be that the slight amount of flux present in the Goldart produces a firmer coat. The addition of a small amount of borax serves the same purpose.

**There is an alternative** to the standard flint/kaolin wash: kyanite, and it contains essentially the same minerals as the standard mix, only Mother Nature has done the mixing. Industry has assisted by grinding the kyanite to 200 mesh, and 0.5% powdered CMC gum helps the wash stick to the kiln shelf. Dry mix the CMC gum with the kyanite before you add water. Kyanite settles rapidly, so only wet mix what you plan to use, and stir as you apply. Sponge your shelves before you continue, and coat quickly with a broad, flat, house-paint brush. The kyanite wash works well at stoneware as well as lower temperatures and may be obtained from the Kyanite Mining Corporation, Dillwyn, Virginia 23936, in 50-pound sacks.

**Instead of kiln wash,** use aluminum foil to cover the kiln floor and shelves. For shelves cut it ¼-inch short of the edge all the way around; the foil pulverizes in the firing and would adhere to any ware on the shelf below if it fell. For use in a top-loading kiln, it is almost necessary to have a small, hand-sized vacuum sweeper in order to clean the kiln thoroughly after each firing. Front-loading kilns can be swept clean with a soft brush.

**In place of liquid kiln wash,** try kaolin. Sprinkle a medium coating of the clay on the floor and each shelf, then load the kiln and fire. There is a small amount of powder present on the bottom of each work after firing, but this washes off easily with water and a sponge after the pots have cooled.

# Plaster

## Mixing and Casting

**If the plaster surface** of your wedging board pits or breaks, the trouble may be with your plaster mixture. When mixing up the plaster for the wedging board, use a denser mixture than for other plaster purposes—2 pounds of plaster to 1 quart of water.

**To eliminate lumps** from plaster which is being mixed for molds, bats, etc., sift it with a flour sifter to remove impurties and hardened particles.

**Store plaster** in airtight containers if you keep it on hand for a long time; otherwise, purchase just enough plaster for your immediate needs.

**Bats can be made stronger** if, when you are casting them, you put a wire coat hanger between two layers of plaster.

**If you add new plaster** to old (perhaps when resurfacing a bat), soak the old plaster thoroughly in water first. Otherwise, the water in the new batch will be absorbed by the old dry plaster with unsatisfactory results. Also, sharply score the old surface before adding the new plaster for a better bond.

**When it is necessary** to work with just a portion of the plaster for a short time before finishing a project (perhaps making sure that all deep-cut areas of the clay model are covered with the first coating of plaster), a portion of the plaster mix can be so handled that it will not set up as quickly as the rest, but will remain soft for the finish work later on: Add the plaster to the water as usual and allow it to slake, then stir the mix just one or two times. Next, pour a portion of the plaster into another bowl and set it aside. If this isn't stirred any more, it will not set up as rapidly as the other portion, which is stirred or mixed constantly until it thickens for use.

**The waxed ½-gallon milk containers** used by the dairies for packaging are excellent for mixing up batches of plaster of Paris. Using these saves the time and trouble of cleaning out mixing bowls, and perhaps may save a plumbing bill. If any plaster is left over after completing a project, it can be left in the carton and discarded. For mixing small batches of plaster, cut the carton down to size before mixing.

**Models for casting molds** of thrown ware may be formed directly on the wheel with the following mixture:

Plaster Throwing Body

| | |
|---|---|
| Kentucky Ball Clay (OM 4) | 14.0% |
| Pottery Plaster (1) | 78.5 |
| Bentonite | 6.0 |
| Sodium Citrate | 1.5 |
| | 100.0% |

Make up only as much of the throwing plaster as will be used in making a single object on the wheel. Mix the dry ingredients and add them to water equivalent to 25% of the weight of the dry ingredients. A little more water may be added as necessary. Wedge the materials thoroughly. The throwing plaster will remain workable for about 20 minutes. This period of time may be extended by increasing the sodium citrate slightly.

**A vibrator**—commonly used for soothing sore muscles— can be used effectively to vibrate a bucket or other container, aiding in eliminating air bubbles when casting plaster.

**To smooth off** plaster bats or molds, a Surform Pocket Plane tool (available in hardware stores) is really good for fast, smooth work; then only fine sandpaper is needed for a good smooth finish. A word of caution: do not use it on wet plaster bats. This tool is also useful for removing scale from kiln shelves.

## Drying Bats

**After soaking old clay scraps** or dry clay, removing excess water is facilitated by allowing the slurry to dry in a concave plaster bat. To pour a concave plaster bat, take a round plastic dishpan and construct a wood box 2 inches wider than the diameter of the pan. Use 1 × 12-inch boards for the sides of the box, and a square of plywood for the bottom. Secure the sides of the box, but do not attach the plywood bottom, then seal the inside joints with coils of moist clay. Paint the interior walls and bottom of the box with liquid soap (as a mold separator), then mix and pour plaster into the box to a depth of 2 inches. As soon as the plaster begins to set, center the dishpan in the box and hold it firmly in place with a gallon bleach bottle full of water. Continue to pour plaster around the dishpan until just below the rim. Allow the plaster to set for several hours, then remove the dishpan and the sides of the box—plywood bottom is left in place to support the uncured plaster and facilitate handling. After the bat has been stored for a week or more, it is ready for use. In addition to its intended use, the bat can be inverted and the bottom used as a solid wedging surface.

**To dry bats and molds,** especially in humid weather, separate the bats with wood slats near the intake of a dehumidifier and cover with a plastic drop cloth.

**Eight- or ten-inch squares** cut from leftover plywood wall paneling make excellent drying bats because they do not warp. Plates, plaques, clay tiles, etc. can be double stacked between the bats, with newspapers between to ease shrinking movement. Plates dry slowly without warping.

**Clay is more satisfactory** for making drying bats than plaster, which will crumble after considerable use and cannot be heated too high for quick drying. Clay bats may be made to any size or shape, then fired to a soft bisque.

**Placing cheesecloth** between wet, drying clay and the plaster bat provides a means of keeping bats clean, and allows easy removal of the clay when it is sufficiently dried. This method is especially useful when small batches of clay of various colors are being prepared for testing. Usually three or four layers of cheesecloth are sufficient to effect drying and prevent clay leakage.

**Occasionally large platters** develop cracks during bisque firing. Rather than accepting a total loss, the platters may be used to reconstitute slip into throwing clay. There are no bits of plaster to worry about getting into the clay, and the porous bisqueware dries the body very quickly. Slip doesn't pass through the crack in the platter because of its thick consistency and the platters are portable enough to be placed wherever there is room.

**To remove excess water** from clay, use newspapers in place of plaster bats to serve the same purpose. Take a 1- or 2-inch-thick pile of newspapers, cover it over with cloth, and then pour the clay slip on the cloth. The cloth keeps the wet newspapers from sticking to the clay and the papers absorb the water very well; in fact, almost as readily as a plaster bat. Newspapers are almost always on hand and the used ones are easily discarded.

## Throwing Bats

**For ease in trimming** flat or recessed lids with high or delicate knobs, cast a thick plaster bat with a 2½-inch-diameter hole in the center. This should allow lids to be inverted, with the hole protecting the knob. Clay lugs will hold the lid in place on the bat.

**Springform cake pans** (available in 7- to 10-inch sizes) make good molds for casting plaster bats. The hardened bats are easily removed by releasing the sides of the pan.

**For potters using a Randall** wheel with a bat head, a useful small bat can be made from a 9-inch pie plate. These fit into the head with enough overhang to be easily picked up. They're easy to make, use less plaster than a standard size, and take up less room on ware boards and in storage.

**Make a chuck on a bat** to facilitate production trimming of mugs. A plaster bat should be first soaked and cleaned thoroughly (it has to be really wet); wooden bats should have three short nails inserted in a triangular configuration near the center. Obtain a paper or plastic drinking cup with wide sloping sides, break out the bottom, center it top down on the bat (over the nails), secure it with clay, and fill it with plaster.

Mugs inverted over the chuck will be in perfect center and may be secured for trimming by tapping on the bottom. This eliminates centering time and adhering with clay; you never have to stop the wheel from one mug to the next.

**To cast a plaster bat,** all you need is a plastic bucket that fits tightly over the wheel head. Cut the bottom off and press the inverted plastic bucket down firmly to seal it from leaks. Mix the plaster and pour. The bat releases from the plastic and the wheel head with no problem. Just make sure your wheel is level and gravity does the rest.

**When casting plaster bats** directly on the wheel head, use a thrown and trimmed band of clay around the outer edge of the head to contain the bat when it is poured. Coat the clay and wheel head with heavy slip or liquid soap before casting. Oily materials should not be used because they stay on the bats and the wheel head and seem to cut down on the absorbency of the plaster.

**Plaster bats** may be cast on the wheel head by wrapping a length of metal shim stock (available in a hardware store) around the edge of the wheel head, and securing it with a large rubber band. Spread Vaseline over the wheel head and along the seam where the shim stock and the wheel head meet, to keep the plaster from sticking. Pour the mixed plaster to whatever depth you want the bat to be, and let it dry. Release the shim stock, and the bat is ready to remove for curing.

**Casting bats** directly on the wheel head is a good method, but the removal of the finished bat can pose problems, despite liberal use of grease or other compounds. A simple solution is to spread a layer of a finely woven, water-saturated cloth over the wheel head before casting. The moist cloth is easily smoothed into place, air bubbles can be forced to the edge if trapped underneath, and the cloth and set-up bat are easily lifted after crystallization of the plaster. Another method is to moisten the wheel head with water or even a little thin slip to produce a somewhat liquid surface. Cover this with a layer of thin plastic such as Saranwrap, and cast plaster on this. The liquid underneath helps to produce a smooth rather than a wrinkled surface.

**To save time,** clay and mess, use clay slip to adhere a removable plaster throwing bat to the wheel head. Put a thick glob of creamy slip on the back of a dry plaster bat, then place the bat slip-side-down on the center of the wheel head. Work the bat in a slight circular fashion until it is securely fastened.

**Instead of installing bat pins** in plaster bats, leave the bottom of the bat plain. To attach the bat, throw a flat plate of clay on the wheel head as if no bat were to be used. Create a spiral depression in the clay by placing the index finger at the center of the clay and pull finger outward while the wheel is moving. With a wet sponge soak the clay "plate" and affix the bat to the clay by moving it back and forth over the wet plate. The suction of the plaster will cause the bat to adhere to the clay. After completion of the pot, pull a wire through the clay just beneath the bat, and you are ready to make another spiral and use another bat. With this method there is no prying of bats from the wheel after throwing, and still there is absolute suction of bat to wheel.

## Nonplaster Bats

**To combine the best qualities** of plaster and Formica-topped particleboard bats, cut rounds from the latter material (an appropriate diameter) and drill bat pin holes to fit your wheel head. With a router, gouge a ½-inch-deep circular area through the Formica into the particleboard disk; the routed diameter should fit just inside the pins (8 to 10 inches). Undercut a recessed edge with a beveled bit; as needed, chisel

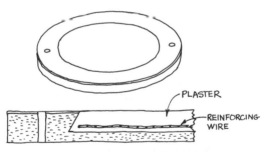

any excess particleboard. Coat the inside of the routed area with liquid plastic or varnish, and allow it to dry. Then place in an X pattern two strips of ¼-inch-mesh screen, 2 inches wide by the diameter of the recess (to serve as reinforcement). Fill with fresh pottery plaster, tap the edge of the bat to eliminate air bubbles and level the top. Allow the bats to cure for a week or so before use. A notch or permanent ink mark at the edge of the bat adjacent to the pin holes aids in easier placement on the wheel head.

**A cabinetmaker** frequently has cutout sections left over from the installation of Formica counter tops. These make excellent large bats or bases on which to build heavy sculpture.

**Companies who manufacture** stereo speakers throw away the rounds that result from cutting holes where the speakers are mounted. These rounds are approximately 10–12 inches in diameter and made of ⅝-inch-thick particleboard; they make excellent throwing bats.

**A 4×8-foot sheet** of Masonite makes twenty-four 12-inch bats, plus some usable drying boards. The Masonite can be cut with a hand-powered keyhole saw, or a saber saw.

**Old 78 rpm phonograph records** make great bats. Their thickness, unlike 33 rpm flexible records, makes them very stable, and the hole in the center of the record facilitates placement on the wheel head. Garage sales are a good place to get 78s; it they are warped, sandwich a few records between two pieces of plywood, with a bag of clay on top for weight, and leave overnight.

**Unmounted Formica**, an excellent material for making throwing bats, can often be obtained as scrap from a cabinet maker.

For a secure bat pin attachment system, drill three ³⁄₁₆-inch holes in the wheel head—two holes exactly opposite one another (about 1 inch in from the edge of the wheel head), and a third hole approximately 2 inches from either of the first two holes (also about 1 inch from the edge of the wheel head). Bats are then drilled with corresponding holes to allow quick alignment and attachment for production throwing. Three 16-penny nails cut to 1½-inch lengths serve as bat pins.

**To eliminate** the plaster problem when throwing pots, use tightly woven canvas disks in place of plaster bats. The dry fabric may be attached with slip and smoothed in place with a rib. Throw a pot on the canvas, then run the wire underneath the cloth bat and carefully slip canvas and pot onto a ware board held level with the wheel head.

**Instead of using plaster bats** on the wheel head, try thin aluminum discs. Made 1 inch smaller than your wheel head, they can be cut with a band saw, and sharp edges sanded smooth.

**The best bats** are clay. Fabricate a plaster mold for bat production, fill with heavily grogged slip, remove and let dry completely before firing to Cone 04.

# Studio Operation

## Cleaning

**A stainless steel scouring pad** is perfect for keeping modeling tools in clean working condition without washing and hence without rusting. Simply brush the tools with the dry pad. Use a wire brush for hard-to-get-at places on plaster cutting tools.

**A quick, easy way to clean** a wheel head, especially one with bat pins, is with a small scrub brush designed for cleaning hands.

**A plastic hairbrush** with widely spaced nylon bristles is excellent for cleaning sticky wet clay from studio tools and utensils (bowls, rolling pins, calipers, etc.). The hairbrush works faster than usual methods, and any clay left in the bristles rinses away quickly.

**Two hand scrapers**, one attached to each side of the splash pan, provide a good way to remove slip from hands before lifting a pot from the wheel. They can be made out of any hard rubber (such as smooth shoe sole neoprene) with a flat edge. Cut the rubber to about 4x3 inches and screw them to the inside of the tray so that ½ inch is above its edge.

**An ice scraper** (the kind used for car windows) is a useful tool for cleaning bats, wedging tables and wheel heads. Some also are equipped with a brush, which is handy for sweeping up dried clay or glaze chemicals.

**When cleaning the studio,** mix a little Calgon in a bucket of warm water. Sponging tables, shelves, etc., with the water picks up clay particles and leaves no streaks or residue.

**Used tea leaves,** collected in a plastic container beside the sink over a few days, make an excellent sweeping compound for the studio floor. Sprinkle them slightly damp. Gardeners can put the final collection on the compost heap.

**To keep dust to a minimum,** keep a plant misting bottle or a regular spray bottle handy. A few quick sprays of water clear the air. It is especially effective over the wedging board.

**In most studios,** where there are potters there are coffee cups. If your studio cups have become stained, put them in the kiln the next time you fire to china-painting temperature, and the cups will come out clean and free of stain.

**Brown spots and stains** on cracked, crazed or chipped porcelain can often be removed by soaking the pot in undiluted Clorox.

**Would you love to throw** pots in a particular room or area but can't because you're afraid of messing up the floor or carpet? A children's molded 4-foot-diameter plastic swimming pool solves the dilemma. Just place the potter's wheel inside and make sure that the legs don't pierce the plastic. (Put a board under sharp metal feet.) All the drips go into the pool along with slurry and clay from your hands. No rubber duckies allowed.

**Thin plastic from the dry cleaner's** is not only perfect for covering ware before firing, it can also serve as an apron while working on the wheel. Slip one cylinder of the plastic over a pants leg and tuck it into your waistband; repeat with the other leg. This should allow freedom to walk around as well as keep legs dry—especially nice in cold weather while traveling to and from the studio.

**In the West,** where cowboy gear is readily available, keep clay off jeans by wearing an old pair of chaps. When the clay dries, it dusts right off with no washing.

**To clean plastic bags** for reuse, wash them in the washing machine. Add a small amount of soap or water softener to the water, then let the machine complete its cycle. Any water trapped inside the bags is shaken out, then the bags are hung upside-down by the corners on the clothesline to dry.

# Energy Savers

**Place strips of Kaowool** (flexible refractory blanket, ½-inch thickness, rated at 2300°F) between the sections of your octagonal electric kiln. This reduces heat loss during firing, insures a slower cooling cycle, and gives a small amount of additional height to the firing chamber.

**To cut as much as an hour** from a bisque or glaze firing, place either a 1-inch-thick blanket of ceramic fiber insulation or old insulating bricks on the lid of your electric kiln.

**To cope with the rising cost** of propane, here is a way to get one-third more pots in the kiln. For a two-burner system with both in the front, flanking the door, the firebox may be shortened to only 16 inches back into the chamber instead of the full width so it occupies much less room. Leave a gap at the junction of the bag wall and the target brick so that flame is directed into the back of the firing chamber. With this method, shelves can be positioned from wall to wall at the rear of the kiln, yet firing temperature should remain even.

**When firing ware** in an electric kiln, why not conserve energy and cook dinner at the same time? Place a pan on the kiln lid and heat any food that requires a long, slow cooking time, such as stew, beans, soup and similar dishes.

**Since typical kiln reduction** can waste gas or oil, throw wood chips through the peepholes at the appropriate time. This extra fuel achieves a reducing atmosphere and compensates for the heat loss common to the reduction phase of firing.

**To conserve kiln space,** try firing small items under inverted hanging planters, making sure that the pots are not touching.

**By referring to the wiring schematic** of an electric kiln equipped with an automatic shut-off device, it is a simple matter to bring two wires out of the control box and attach them to an electric clock for monitoring the duration of a firing. The clock is activated when the kiln is turned on, and stopped when the automatic switch shuts off the current. By logging the time lapse, it is thus easy to check kilowatt hour consumption and watch more accurately for irregularities.

143

**In sunnier areas** of the world, placing kiln furniture and greenware in the sun for three or four hours before loading and lighting burners may decrease bisque firing time by up to two hours. With a small gas kiln it is possible and convenient to "solar heat," load and fire in one day.

## Health and Safety

**To avoid cracked and reddened hands** from constant contact with clay, try throwing with rubber gloves from the hardware store. Transparent and strong, they are inexpensive enough to be discarded after three or four sessions.

**Disposable vinyl gloves** used by physicians are excellent protection for hands when throwing with heavily grogged clay. The only change in the throwing process is that a bit more water is needed for lubrication. These gloves may be the answer for extended periods of throwing rough clay, and may also help people with skin allergies that are affected by clay contact. The gloves come in three sizes and are so thin that they allow almost complete sensitivity of touch, and yet they will not break from friction with rough grog.

**Toy balloons** provide excellent protection for cuts and abrasions while throwing. Be sure to cut off the open end as this coil tends to impede circulation. The balloons work very well over bandaged areas, and allow continuous production.

**Wrap a small piece of cotton cloth** around an injured finger when throwing with gritty clay.

**Here is a simple remedy** for overly dry hands: After finishing work and washing your hands, apply a generous coat of cider vinegar. Let this dry, then add a second coat. The alkaline content of clay dries out the skin and the acetic acid (vinegar) counteracts this.

**To clean hands** after throwing without washing them, keep a piece of burlap handy to use as a rag. It readily absorbs water and slip, and it scrapes off partially hardened clay.

**To alleviate the problem** of damaging fingernails and/or tips of fingers while throwing, glue a fake fingernail onto the jeopardized finger. It does not slip off while throwing, yet is easily removed.

144

**Using a bat** on the wheel head may change your position enough to make throwing unfamiliar and uncomfortable. But placing the same size bat on the chair restores your accustomed position.

**Placing two bricks** on the floor under your left foot when throwing on a portable electric wheel raises the left knee to hip level and reduces strain on the back.

**Leather welding gloves** are useful for raku. They wear better than asbestos, and are more easily obtained (at welding shops in local communities). Asbestos gloves will burn when frayed along the edges, while leather gloves are not readily inclined to fray.

**To prevent burning your arms** while lifting objects out of the raku kiln, cut the sleeves from an old leather jacket and staple them to asbestos gloves. The leather reflects heat and does not char.

**Scraps of an old,** thick, pure wool blanket are a good substitute for asbestos gloves when handling spy hole plugs, etc., during firing. Although they singe a bit at times, they will not burst into flames.

## Heat

**To avoid working with cold clay,** cover the clay stockpile with an old electric blanket and turn up the control the night before you plan to throw. Nothing like nice warm clay on a cold winter day.

**A simple, inexpensive heater** may be purchased at most hardware household departments to keep your throwing water warm. They are designed to warm water instantly for coffee, etc.

**For those who work in the cold,** an aquarium heater keeps the throwing water nice and toasty.

**If your kiln** has a "duty" cycle—that is, the low setting produces heat intermittently—it can be a valuable warming device for the studio. During a cold winter, turning the kiln on low can keep the workshop from freezing. For a 10-hour period, it should be for a total of approximately one hour, providing the needed, minimal warmth without a high electric bill.

**For the potter** who prefers to pot outside, but finds weather conditions often uncomfortably cool, look for a discarded floor lamp at a Salvation Army or Goodwill shop to insure being warm. The best lamp for this purpose is one with a heavily weighted base, a vertical pole, and three bullet-shaped lamp holders that swivel. It is generally the swiveling action of these individual lamps that fails, and is responsible for the lamp being cast off. These generally can be inexpensively repaired and, instead of using regular bulbs, insert two or three of the "infra-red" variety. As these bulbs have wider diameters, simply take a pair of tin snips and remove most of the thin metal shade to accommodate the larger bulb. A floor lamp thus equipped, standing near the wheel, will guarantee your being toasty warm.

## Organization

**To file glaze recipes** without fumbling through a file box a class record book (used in public schools) will hold three $3 \times 5$ cards per page. On each card record the glaze ingredients and mark them with a code highlighted by underlining as to matt, smooth, stony, etc. Placing tape across the top of the cards will allow them to be flipped, and notes may be recorded on the back. In addition, the front of the book may be used for glaze and ceramic materials inventory so everything is compact and in one place. It lies flat and the ruled lines and pages make the job of organizing much easier.

**To avoid missing** an exhibition entry deadline and not getting slides mailed for jurying on time, a $3 \times 5$-inch card file works well and helps eliminate the stack of publications listing workshops or shows. On each file card paste a clipping from columns such as CM's "Where to Show," and file by deadline. Because many events are annual affairs, it's a good idea to include additional information about a particular exhibition, such as the names of artists nearby who might share transporting artwork next year.

**As your stack** of CM magazines grows, it becomes increasingly difficult to locate information. Now, when you read something that you may want to refer to again, note it and the page number on the cover, It is no longer necessary to thumb through many magazines to find that elusive bit of information.

**Many potters** use several different stoneware clays that when bisqued often look much alike. To keep track of which clay was used (since glazes often look better on one body than another), put a code letter under the signature on the bottom of the pot. If it's a mixture of clays, just put an X. This, of course, is also useful in identifying finished work.

**A one-character clay body code** and two-character glaze code eliminate the usual scribbling and use of abbreviations on test tiles. Each clay body is assigned an arbitrary capital letter, A through Z; for more than 26 clay bodies double the letters AA, AB, AC. (The clay code is carved into the tile when leather-hard to positively identify the body and eliminate questions as to which was used with the glaze.) Each glaze and slip is assigned an alphabetical letter and numeral, such as A1, M14, S4, Z12; oxides and colorants may also be assigned a lower case letter code, such as c for copper carbonate, r for rutile, ri for red iron oxide. Such coding can even identify glazes over glazes: A2-r7-M16 indicates glaze A2 with an addition of 7% rutile, applied over glaze M16.

**To keep track of the glazes** on pots in the event they are chipped during stacking of the glaze kiln, make penciled notations on the bottom of each pot—e.g. H.W. for Hoover's White. This is simply and quickly done, and burns out during firing.

**With the need** to employ efficient processes in the studio, a card file containing type of production item, weight of clay, finished dimensions and raw dimensions should be particularly useful for those items which have been phased out of your current production line (and current memory) and then reordered.

# Storage

**Small holes** drilled in a surface convenient to your work area make good holders for needle tools. Multiple holes afford a much better chance of hitting one when you want to set your tool aside, yet they do not damage the surface or preclude its use for other purposes.

**Nail a small sponge** on a board in front of your wheel; needle tools can be stuck in for quick access.

**Clay tools can be stored** in inexpensive plastic silverware organizers, and the tools can be easily seen in them. Buy several and stack them for extra space.

**Instead of using the sink** or a box as a "catch-all basin" for sponges, devise a rack for holding them and to enable keeping a check on the number of sponges always available for immediate use: The sponge rack should be constructed over a sink

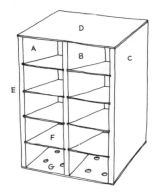

so that excess water from the damp sponges may drip harmlessly into the sink, not onto the floor. In the diagram, A-B-C shows side walls made from 1-inch wood stock. D is aluminum sheeting attached to the top, back and bottom. E shows grooves cut into side walls at a 15° angle. F shows aluminum shelves cut to fit into the grooves. Finally, G shows ¼-inch holes drilled in the aluminum to allow water to drain out of the rack.

The overall size of the rack depends upon the size and number of damp sponges to be stored.

**If keeping tools handy** and within easy reach while throwing is a problem, construct a tool rack by enclosing two scrub brushes in a wood frame. Face the stiff-bristled surfaces together, overlapping the bristles about ½ inch, then build a frame from 1 × 3 lumber to hold them in place. The bristles will hold the handles of tools firmly and each individual tool will be clearly visible.

**Make several clay pocket-type** containers to hang on the wall over the workbench as holders for tools, paintbrushes, pencils or sponges. They afford a practical and decorative means of keeping materials handy.

**Potters can use disposable** "baby wipes" containers for holding water-soluble wax resist. Cut away the loose plastic flaps underneath the small snap-on lid to expose an orifice large enough to accept a brush for waxing. The snap-on lid still functions between uses to seal the container which can be marked with the name of its contents using a felt-tipped marker after the original label is peeled away.

**No more broken stilts** when you take a piece of corrugated cardboard, about 2 feet square, and push your stilts into it. The cardboard may be hung on the wall above or near the kiln. Use a section of coat hanger wire to fashion a hook and place it in the center top of the cardboard.

**Leather-hard spouts,** handles and lids can be stored indefinitely in Ziploc plastic bags. Thus, an extra part is always ready for attachment to a teapot, mug or other multiple-element ware.

**Cardboard drums,** often used for shipment of glaze chemicals, can be employed in numerous ways by the studio potter. They may be covered with burlap or painted, packed with pots, and taken to craft fairs or other informal exhibits. When unpacked, they make attractive display props.

**To avoid knocking over tiny vials** of gold, luster or over-glaze while they are being used, nail some deep bottle caps (like ketchup caps) open end up to a thin board a few inches wide. Each vial can be placed in its own holder and is not only protected from being knocked over but also leans toward the user at a convenient angle.

**When working with lusters,** metals, or other materials that come in small bottles, it is all too easy to overturn the bottles and waste the material. If these small bottles are embedded in a wad of clay while in use, accidents can be avoided.

# Ceramic Raw Materials

| Material | Formula | Molecular Weight | Equivalent Weight | Fired Formula |
|---|---|---|---|---|
| Aluminum Hydroxide | $Al_2(OH)_6$ | 156 | 156 | $Al_2O_3$ |
| Barium Carbonate | $BaCO_3$ | 197 | 197 | $BaO$ |
| Bone Ash | $Ca_3(PO_4)_2$ | 310 | 103 | $CaO$ |
| Borax | $Na_2O \cdot 2B_2O_3 \cdot 10H_2O$ | 382 | 382 | $Na_2O \cdot 2B_2O_3$ |
| Boric Acid | $B_2O_3 \cdot 3H_2O$ | 124 | 124 | $B_2O_3$ |
| Colemanite (Calcium Borate) | $2CaO \cdot 3B_2O_3 \cdot 5H_2O$ | 412 | 206 | $2CaO \cdot 3B_2O_3$ |
| Cryolite | $Na_3AlF_6$ | 210 | 420 | $3Na_2O \cdot Al_2O_3$ |
| Dolomite | $CaCO_3 \cdot MgCO_3$ | 184 | 184 | $CaO \cdot MgO$ |
| Feldspar, Potash (theoretical) | $K_2O \cdot Al_2O_3 \cdot 6SiO_2$ | 557 | 557 | same |
| Feldspar, Soda (theoretical) | $Na_2O \cdot Al_2O_3 \cdot 6SiO_2$ | 524 | 524 | same |
| Flint (Silica, Quartz) | $SiO_2$ | 60 | 60 | same |
| Fluorspar | $CaF_2$ | 78 | 78 | $CaO$ |
| Kaolin (China Clay) | $Al_2O_3 \cdot 2SiO_2 \cdot 2H_2O$ | 258 | 258 | $Al_2O_3 \cdot 2SiO_2$ |
| Lead, Red | $Pb_3O_4$ | 684 | 228 | $PbO$ |
| Lead, White | $2PbCO_3 \cdot Pb(OH)_2$ | 775 | 258 | $PbO$ |
| Lead, Yellow (Litharge) | $PbO$ | 223 | 223 | same |
| Lepidolite | $LiF \cdot KF \cdot Al_2O_3 \cdot 3SiO_2$ | 356 | 356 | same |
| Lithium Carbonate | $Li_2CO_3$ | 74 | 74 | $Li_2O$ |
| Magnesium Carbonate | $MgCO_3$ | 84 | 84 | $MgO$ |
| Pearl Ash | $K_2CO_3$ | 138 | 138 | $K_2O$ |
| Petalite | $Li_2O \cdot Al_2O_3 \cdot 8SiO_2$ | 197 | 197 | same |
| Pyrophyllite | $Al_2O_3 \cdot 4SiO_2 \cdot H_2O$ | 360 | 360 | $Al_2O_3 \cdot 4SiO_2$ |
| Soda Ash | $Na_2CO_3$ | 106 | 106 | $Na_2O$ |
| Sodium Bicarbonate | $NaHCO_3$ | 84 | 168 | $Na_2O$ |
| Spodumene | $Li_2O \cdot Al_2O_3 \cdot 4SiO_2$ | 372 | 372 | same |
| Strontium Carbonate | $SrCO_3$ | 148 | 148 | $SrO$ |
| Talc | $3MgO \cdot 4SiO_2 \cdot H_2O$ | 379 | 126 | $3MgO \cdot 4SiO_2$ |
| Tin Oxide | $SnO_2$ | 151 | 151 | same |
| Titanium Dioxide | $TiO_2$ | 80 | 80 | same |
| Whiting | $CaCO_3$ | 100 | 100 | $CaO$ |
| Wollastonite | $Ca \cdot SiO_3$ | 116 | 116 | same |
| Zinc Oxide | $ZnO$ | 81 | 81 | same |
| Zircopax | $ZrO_2 \cdot SiO_2$ | 183 | 183 | same |
| Zirconium Oxide | $ZrO_2$ | 123 | 123 | same |

## Colorants

| Material | Formula | Molecular Weight | Equivalent Weight | Fired Formula |
|---|---|---|---|---|
| Chromic Oxide | $Cr_2O_3$ | 152 | 152 | same |
| Cobalt Carbonate | $CoCO_3$ | 119 | 119 | $CoO$ |
| Cobalt Oxide, Black | $Co_3O_4$ | 241 | 80 | $CoO$ |
| Copper Carbonate | $CuCO_3$ | 124 | 124 | $CuO$ |
| Copper Oxide (Cupric) | $CuO$ | 80 | 80 | same |
| Copper Oxide (Cuprous) | $Cu_2O$ | 143 | 80 | $CuO$ |
| Iron Chromate | $FeCrO_4$ | 172 | 172 | same |
| Iron Oxide, Red (Ferric) | $Fe_2O_3$ | 160 | 160 | same |
| Iron Oxide, Black (Ferrous) | $FeO$ | 72 | 72 | same |
| Manganese Carbonate | $MnCO_3$ | 115 | 115 | $MnO$ |
| Manganese Dioxide, Black | $MnO_2$ | 87 | 87 | same |
| Nickel Oxide, Green | $NiO$ | 75 | 75 | same |
| Nickel Oxide, Black | $Ni_2O_3$ | 166 | 83 | $NiO$ |
| Rutile (Titanium Dioxide, Impure) | $TiO_2$ | 80 | 80 | same |

# Temperature Equivalents for Orton Standard Pyrometric Cones

| Cone Number | Large Cones 150°C* | 270°F* | Cone Number | Small Cones 300°C* | 540°F* |
|---|---|---|---|---|---|
| 022 | 586 | 1086 | 022 | 630 | 1165 |
| 021 | 614 | 1137 | 021 | 643 | 1189 |
| 020 | 635 | 1175 | 020 | 666 | 1231 |
| 019 | 683 | 1261 | 019 | 723 | 1333 |
| 018 | 717 | 1323 | 018 | 752 | 1386 |
| 017 | 747 | 1377 | 017 | 784 | 1443 |
| 016 | 792 | 1458 | 016 | 825 | 1517 |
| 015 | 804 | 1479 | 015 | 843 | 1549 |
| 014 | 838 | 1540 | 014 | 870 | 1596 |
| 013 | 852 | 1566 | 013 | 880 | 1615 |
| 012 | 884 | 1623 | 012 | 900 | 1650 |
| 011 | 894 | 1641 | 011 | 915 | 1680 |
| 010 | 894 | 1641 | 010 | 919 | 1686 |
| 09 | 923 | 1693 | 09 | 955 | 1751 |
| 08 | 955 | 1751 | 08 | 983 | 1801 |
| 07 | 984 | 1803 | 07 | 1008 | 1846 |
| 06 | 999 | 1830 | 06 | 1023 | 1873 |
| 05 | 1046 | 1915 | 05 | 1062 | 1944 |
| 04 | 1060 | 1940 | 04 | 1098 | 2008 |
| 03 | 1101 | 2014 | 03 | 1131 | 2068 |
| 02 | 1120 | 2048 | 02 | 1148 | 2098 |
| 01 | 1137 | 2079 | 01 | 1178 | 2152 |
| 1 | 1154 | 2109 | 1 | 1179 | 2154 |
| 2 | 1162 | 2124 | 2 | 1179 | 2154 |
| 3 | 1168 | 2134 | 3 | 1196 | 2185 |
| 4 | 1186 | 2167 | 4 | 1209 | 2208 |
| 5 | 1196 | 2185 | 5 | 1221 | 2230 |
| 6 | 1222 | 2232 | 6 | 1255 | 2291 |
| 7 | 1240 | 2264 | 7 | 1264 | 2307 |
| 8 | 1263 | 2305 | 8 | 1300 | 2372 |
| 9 | 1280 | 2336 | 9 | 1317 | 2403 |
| 10 | 1305 | 2381 | 10 | 1330 | 2426 |
| 11 | 1315 | 2399 | 11 | 1336 | 2437 |
| 12 | 1326 | 2419 | 12 | 1355 | 2471 |

*Degree of temperature rise per hour.

# Kiln Atmosphere Colors and Corresponding Temperatures (Approximate)

| Color | Cone | °F | °C |
|-------|------|-----|-----|
| Dull Red Glow | 022 | 1080 | 580 |
| Dark Red | 019 | 1220 | 660 |
| Cherry Red | 014 | 1530 | 830 |
| Red-Orange | 010 | 1680 | 915 |
| Orange | 05 | 1900 | 1040 |
| Yellow-Orange | 1 | 2120 | 1160 |
| Yellow | 4 | 2170 | 1185 |
| Yellow-White | 6 | 2250 | 1230 |
| White | 10 | 2380 | 1305 |
| Brilliant White | 15 | 2600 | 1425 |
| Dazzling White | 20 | 2800 | 1540 |

## Temperature Conversion

To convert a Centigrade temperature to Fahrenheit multiply the temperature by 9/5 and add 32:
100°C x 9/5 = 180 + 32 = 212°F

To convert Fahrenheit to Centigrade subtract 32 and multiply the answer by 5/9:
212°F − 32 = 180 x 5/9 = 100°C